# CRISIS

# IN CANDYLAND

# CRISIS IN CANDYLAND

## Melting the Chocolate Shell of the Mars Family Empire

JAN POTTKER

An Enigma Book

National Press Books

 Published in the United States by National Press Books, Inc. Quantity discounts are available from the Special Sales Department, National Press Books, 7200 Wisconsin Avenue, Bethesda, MD 20814; (800) 275-8888.



Library of Congress Cataloging-in-Publication Data

Pottker, Janice
Crisis in Candyland
melting the chocolate shell of the Mars family empire
Jan Pottker
256 p. 15 x 23 cm
Includes index.
ISBN 1-882605-20-9
1. Mars, Incorporated.
2. Food industry and trade—United States—Case studies.
I. Title.
HD9009.M27P68 1995
338.7'664'00973—dc20

95-17557
CIP

PRINTED IN THE UNITED STATES OF AMERICA

10 9 8 7 6 5 4 3 2 1

*To my sister Mary Heléne Pottker Rosenbaum,*
*with great love and admiration.*

# Acknowledgments

Alan Sultan of National Press Books has been my enthusiastic supporter and advocate throughout the research and writing, and I thank him for his support as well as that of my publisher, Joel Joseph. My sister, Mary Heléne Rosenbaum of Black Bear Productions, Inc., gave me editorial assistance that was of a substance and quality well beyond that which writers ordinarily receive. For this, and other reasons, I have dedicated *Crisis in Candyland* to her. My agent Marcy Posner, vice president of William Morris Agency, provided publishing acumen and was a mainstay throughout this project. I also want to thank Eric Zohn, who reviewed and revised my contract with great skill. And thank you to Krystl Hall, also of William Morris Agency.

Without the terrific research assistance given by Catherine O'Donnell, this book could not have been completed on a timely basis. Cathy dropped other projects whenever I needed her and, like me, would obsess until she found the reference we needed. Olga Somenzi Pottker, my mother, also provided research help as she has continued to do for all of my books. I was also given valuable research assistance by Daniel Fernandez.

The library staff of Library of Congress went out of their way to assist me at any time I needed them, in particular the staff in the Periodicals Room in the Madison Building and in the Business Reference Room in the Adams Building. I also appreciate the facilities of Montgomery County, Maryland, Public Libraries, Montgomery College in Rockville, Maryland and McKeldin Library, University of Maryland, College Park. For reasons which I state in the Preface, I will not name those people who work or are consultants to the Mars companies or are employed by the family. You know who you are and I thank you. In the confectionery industry, I would like to thank: Ken Wolfe, CEO and chairman of Hershey Foods Inc.; Bonnie Glass Hinkson of Hershey Foods Inc.; François Perroud, assistant vice president for Press Information of Nestlé SA; Tricia Bowles of Nestlé USA; Ellen Gordon, president of Tootsie Roll Industries,Inc.; Mary Wills of Tootsie Roll; Mark Andrews of Andrews Associates Inc.; Lisa Huse of The Procter & Gamble Company; Susan Smith of Chocolate Manufacturers of the USA and National Confectioner's Association; Lisbeth Echeandia of *Confectionery Magazine;* and Chrissy Farrell of Advanstar Communications.

I would also like to thank Sally Sturm, librarian, Mars Public Library, Mars, Pennsylvania; John K. Gott of the Fahquier Heritage Society, Marshall, Virginia; Bob Sinclair of Hunt Country Tours, Fahquier County, Virginia; and staff at the Thomas Balch Library, Leesburg, Virginia. Thanks go to the American Dental Association and to Michael Jacobson of the Center for Science in the Public Interest and to the matrimonial unit clerks at Somerset County, New Jersey, Courthouse.

Thanks also go to Richard H. Singer Jr. of Skoloff & Wolfe, Livingston, New Jersey and to Joel Kobert of Courter, Kobert, Laufer, Purcell & Cohen of Morristown, New Jersey. I send a special thank you to Harold A. Vogel, Jr.

Thanks also go to Professor Richard Berezden of American University, Austin Kiplinger of The Kiplinger Washington Editors, Inc., Tom Delaney of *The Delaney Report,* New York City, Garry Clifford and Peter Meyer of *People* magazine, and to Frankie Welch of Frankie Welch Designs, Alexandria, Virginia. My close friend M. Kathleen McCulloch listened, daily, to my tales of the Mars family and I appreciate her patience and her friendship. Doreen Conrad offered the advice and support that only another writer can provide, as did Dan Moldea and Fiona Houston. I also want to thank Eleanor Baker, Steven Brady, Louise Edeiken, David Gibbs, Larry Greenbaum, David Hochberg, Terri Krueger, Nanci Nathan, Ned Rosenbaum, William Rosenbaum, Ed Stern, Linda Stern, Catharine Staats Taubman, and Duncan Wood for his singing rendition of the Smarties jingle. Also to Tonus Studio of Potomac, Maryland for keeping me healthy and fit during this project.

My heartfelt appreciation goes to my husband, Andrew S. Fishel, for his editorial judgment and personal sustenance. Although my older daughter, Tracy Pottker-Fishel, was at college during this project, I appreciate her continued interest. Carrie Pottker-Fishel deserves special thanks for bearing with her mother through yet another deadline.

# *Contents*

# Preface

# The Mars Family and Company

Candy. It runs like a bright peppermint stripe through our culture. Christmas stockings are stuffed with it, young lovers proffer it in gorgeous velvet and satin Valentine boxes, the Easter Bunny brings baskets of it, children go door-to-door begging for it at Halloween. Sweets are a reward for good behavior, a comfort under stress, a pick-me-up when energy flags. We worry about fat and calories, but the naughtiness of candy is low on the calendar of sins compared to drugs, alcohol, unsafe sex, and the rest of the dismal modern catalogue of dangers. What could be more all-American, more redolent of Andy Hardy towns and wholesome kids, than a candy bar?

Intrigue, secrecy, and repression seem utterly alien to the flavor of candy. If we vaguely know that our sweets are not being produced by a genial Willie Wonka, we still don't think of the families who manufacture candy as being in the domain of the Addams family. But the planet Mars itself is not farther from Candyland than the Mars family is from warmhearted Willie Wonka.

Across the Potomac River from Washington, D.C. is an unobtrusive, red-brick structure in the quiet suburb of McLean, Virginia. The office building sits on a tree-lined road aptly named Elm Street. Although the architecture has no obtrusive characteristics, a pedestrian giving it a second glance would notice that the design is dark and fortress-like. The edifice does not include large windows, skylights or anything else that would let in either the sun or a glimpse of the interior to outsiders. In fact, there's not even a sign visible from the street that identifies the activity housed within.

This building is the headquarters of Mars, Inc., one of the country's—and perhaps the world's—most secretive businesses. The building serves as a metaphor for the Mars business and family: confining and cold.

Three miles away lies the nation's top security operation, the Central Intelligence Agency. Mars, which enforces a vow of secrecy on every person who works for it, has often been compared to the CIA. This analogy is overstated. Mars, Inc. is far better at keeping its operations secret than the CIA.

A private family business, Mars, Inc. is no mom-and-pop operation. Its reach is global: it has 52 plants in 31 countries, and 28,000 employees. Mars products are sold in China and Eastern bloc countries as well as South Africa. It is the fifth largest private company in the United States, and is ninety-fourth in size overall, with worldwide revenues estimated at $12.5 billion in 1994. Its major subsidiaries are M&M/Mars (candy), Kal Kan Foods, Inc. (pet food) and Uncle Ben's, Inc. (rice). It also manufactures ice cream and snack foods, and owns an electronic products company.

Several of its candies, including Snickers candy bar and M&M's Plain and Peanut Chocolate Candies, have been among the top ten confections in the United States for decades.

The company was founded in the early 1920s by Frank Mars, who manufactured the popular Milky Way, Mars Almond, Snickers and 3 Musketeers candy bars. His son, Forrest E. Sr., now 91, brought its brands to the United Kingdom in the 1930s, where he also began a pet food empire. In the United States, Forrest established M&M's candies and Uncle Ben's rice. In 1964, nearly 30 years after Frank's death, Forrest combined his businesses with his father's, to form Mars, Inc. Forrest's businesses had grown significantly larger than Frank's American candy company, generating sales four times as great and assets more than double his father's.

In 1973, Forrest virtually gave the company to his three children: Forrest Jr., now 64, John, 59, and Jackie, 54. At that time, the business had $500 million in sales and no debt. The brothers have spent their entire careers in the company; Jackie has become more active in the last decade, when the company began to suffer serious reversals. The three siblings have ten children among them, seven of whom have worked for Mars, Inc.

*Crisis in Candyland* is the story of the Mars family and of their multinational company. It is the only book to be written and published on this company and the family who owns it.

As I began research on the Mars company and the Mars family, I knew my task of uncovering the story behind the country's largest candy company would be challenging. Ambitious tasks don't frighten me, however: I have a Ph.D. from Columbia University that was invaluable in teaching me social analysis and research methods. These skills helped me uncover the true story of the world's most popular advice columnists for an earlier book. My unauthorized biography of Ann Landers and Abigail Van Buren, published in 1987, was *Dear Ann, Dear Abby.* Taking on these two formidable ladies and their syndicates was an unnerving job due to their influence and power.

In 1992, I published *Born to Power*, which profiled 50 young heirs to such prominent businesses as Koch Oil and Levi Strauss. I analyzed their business styles and elicited insights about their family relationships.

In researching my books and articles, I've run across more than my share of large corporations that stonewall, equivocate and deny.

But I wasn't prepared for Mars, Inc.

I should have been forewarned by a 1986 article on the company that appeared in the Washington, DC business magazine *Regardie's*. The feature was as much about how difficult it is for a writer to gain entry to the company as it was about the company itself. Surprisingly, the writer was Ron Kessler, author of the best-selling *Inside the White House* and a man who has successfully exposed secrets of the FBI, the CIA and the KGB. Yet he couldn't fully crack open the candy shell of Mars, Inc.

I wasn't sure that I could, either.

I had heard of a middle-school student in Atlanta who wrote Mars, Inc. in 1986, as part of a school project, to ask how the Milky Way candy bar got its name. The company responded to the sixth-grader that the information was "classified and confidential." And when *The Wall Street Journal* followed up, the company refused to "even divulge the name of the Mars official who would issue a comment if a comment were to be issued."

A writer from the magazine *The Nation* called the company and found he also wasn't to be given answers even to basic questions. He wrote, "'Well,' I sighed, 'I've always heard that M&M/Mars is discreet. It is discreet, isn't it?'

'I'm afraid I can't comment on that,' responded the Mars spokesperson."

Not only outsiders end up feeling angry at Mars. I was surprised, for example, when I contacted former Mars executives who, at first, demurred from interviews because talking about the company brought back too many unpleasant memories. They just wanted to forget. "I want to put Mars behind me," said one.

My approach to the company itself was a formal request for information and interviews with managers. I knew there was no point raising, at that early date, the suggestion of an interview with the Mars family members themselves, who are well known for never speaking to the press, on or off the record.

Employees of the company are told that if they talk to the press, they will be dismissed. After the abrupt firing of one company president in the early 80s, rumors circulated that the reason was his talking to the press. Whether or not his indiscretion was the cause of his dismissal, it served as a cold warning to other Mars staff.

Indeed, as I called advertising agency staff and business consultants who had worked on Mars accounts for interviews—people who were not even necessarily working with Mars, Inc. at that moment—I heard fearful answers. "No," most everyone said. "I might want to work with the company in the future." My promise of anonymity did not always persuade them to change their minds. "It doesn't matter if you don't use my name," said one man. "They'll still find out. They have their ways."

At first, I thought these responses were ludicrous. After all, United States senators, heads of newspaper syndicates and the largest companies' chief executive officers have had conversations with me that were off the record. Yet I learned that when unfavorable articles with anonymous quotations about the Mars company appear in the news, Forrest Jr. and John will try to figure out who talked. They even call in other executives to help them brainstorm and pin blame. And as one Mars associate told me, "they are punitive" whether or not their guess as to who talked is correct.

In fact, I had contacted the attorney, Joseph "Chip" Volpe III, who represented Virginia Mars in her 1990 divorce from Forrest Jr. Although Volpe's representation of Virginia is a matter of public record, when called he said that he would "neither confirm nor deny" that he had represented her. Such is the feeling that the Mars family instills in anyone whom they employ.

As a result, I have decided to protect people in my acknowledgments. I have thanked only people outside the company: not those who are employed by Mars, who have been employed by Mars or whose businesses work with the company. In good conscience, it is just too risky to name the few who did not think to ask for anonymity because they might be blamed for comments they had not made, causing the wrath of the god Mars to come down on them.

Several times in the past 15 years, the company has become uncharacteristically sensitive over the hostile image it is given in the media. To counteract the public's negative perception of Mars, the metropolitan Washington company twice—in 1981 and 1992—allowed *The Washington Post* limited access to the company. Interviews with some of its managers were granted and, in 1992, the writer was allowed into the Mars headquarters building and a manufacturing plant. But soon after the 1992 story appeared, the company regretted its moment of openness; although the piece was not critical, the Mars brothers were furious that the writer had brought up some of the company's—and the family's—more embarrassing moments. Mars now sees this episode as a momentary lapse in judgment and it will not allow a writer access any time in the near future.

National Press Books, my publisher, was interested in buying the photos from the freelance photographer who had been allowed into Mars manufacturing plants to shoot the pictures accompanying the 1992 *Post* piece. The photographer laughed.

"The photos aren't available," he told us. "Mars was so unhappy about the story that they bought photo rights from me for a king's ransom so no other writer could use the pictures."

Of course, a book focusing on a leading candy company cannot be written without gaining the point of view of management from competitive candy businesses. In each case, I received professional cooperation from such companies as Hershey Foods Corporation, Nestlé SA and Tootsie Roll Industries. Although not even the lowest-level employee of Mars was allowed to speak with me, for example, I was granted a lengthy interview with Kenneth L. Wolfe, president and chairman of Hershey, who talked with me about the industry, about Hershey and about its place relative to Mars, Inc. I also spoke with Ellen Gordon, president of Tootsie Roll, and François Perroud, vice president of Nestlé.

I did expect, incorrectly as it turns out, that the Mars company would be interested in my offer to allow them to fact-check this book. That way, the "external affairs" office of Mars, as it calls itself, would be able to counter any item they perceived as inaccurate and would be able to communicate their own point of view. I also thought they'd like an early peek at the book—a book that would reveal, like nothing ever written before, the inner secrets of this company and the family that runs it. By seeing the book's manuscript before publication, they'd have more time to begin their efforts at damage control and spin.

Instead, they advised me that "due to the extensive demands on our time, we are simply unable to provide assistance to anyone writing about our business."

I assume they'll take time now to read this book.

Through many interviews and follow-up conversations with people who have worked for Mars, Inc., with personal employees of the Mars family or with those who were intimates of key Mars family members, a surprising tale of one of the largest, richest family business dynasties in this country emerges.

*Crisis in Candyland* portrays a family that is cold, controlling and autocratic: one that runs its business the same way it treats family members. The dysfunctions of the older generations are not only passed on to current Mars relatives but have become the legacy of the company as well. As the business tries to meet new challenges in global markets from larger multinational companies, the personal characteristics of its leaders make it questionable whether Mars can react as flexibly as it must do to remain competitive.

The company's refusal to allow the use of M&M's in the movie *E.T.*, for example, is typical of how the company's managers are so out-of-touch and fearful of making a mistake that they will veto a good idea. Mars' misjudgment allowed Hershey to jump in and offer Steven Spielberg the use of Reese's Pieces candy for his lovable extraterrestrial creature: sales shot up 70 percent as a result.

But the family's insistence on controlling all decisions and distrusting the professional opinions of even its managers has hurt the company terribly. Not that any of the Marses are open to colleagues or friends at any level: Jackie, for example, refuses to fill out the alumnae questionnaire sent her annually by *Bryn Mawr College,* for fear of disclosing personal information about herself. And no Mars family member will agree to have a photo taken for publication.

While Forrest Mars Sr. has only given one interview in his life, he does like to talk. He will lean forward, I have been told, and speak intensely, usually clutching and squeezing his listener's arm as he makes his point. Some of these conversations, in turn, were repeated to me.

Despite the popular belief that the main ambition of Forrest Mars Sr. was to establish a family dynasty, I found—through my interviews of those who have talked to him about his family—that this is untrue. Forrest, who is presumably nearing the end of his long life, is not—repeat, is not—bent on having the Mars company stay in the family. In fact, his early—and sole—interview, given to a trade publication in 1966, serves to support his current lack of interest in keeping Mars, Inc. a dynastic family business.

Some of his ambivalence, I learned, is due to his deep concern over the way the company is losing shares in its markets all over the world. He questions the ability of his sons, Forrest Jr. and John, to ensure Mars' prominence in the candy industry. As I quote him in this book, he has said of his sons, "They think they can't run it into the ground, but they can." Nor does he put much faith in the younger Mars generation, his grandchildren.

Shortly after beginning this book, after I had been refused access to the company, I received an odd piece of mail from Mars, Inc. Inside the company's envelope was a short pamphlet, presumably written for schoolchildren, on the history of the company's products.

Accompanying the brochure were two fifty cent coupons, good for discounts on Mars candy products.

Throughout the extensive research, interviews and writing that I did for this book, those coupons are the only form of assistance provided me by Mars, Inc.

But, in the words of the legendary Forrest Mars Sr., "Nothing worthwhile really comes easy."

# One

# The Founder: Franklin (Frank) C. Mars

On September 24, 1883, Franklin C. Mars was born into a setting as linked to America's traditional image of itself as any Frank Capra movie set: the small town of Newport near the Wisconsin border outside St. Paul, Minnesota. Frank's mother was a member of the Holten family, pioneer settlers of Minnesota—from the world of Babbitt and boosterism, of Garrison Keillor's Lake Wobegon and the sturdy virtues of the frontier.

On the other side of the family tree, Frank would say that his father was a descendent of the founder of Mars, Pennsylvania, which is located in the western region of that state, north of Pittsburgh. However, this story—like many other officially sanctioned Mars legends—is completely untrue. Local Pennsylvania historians link the name of the town, founded circa 1873, either to the planet Mars, or to an early farming family named Marshall.

Although Frank boasted about his parents' long American lineage, neither one was well-off. Frank's father had moved to Minnesota from Pennsylvania so that he could find employment in one of the many gristmills that served the state's emerging flour industry. Fourteen years earlier, Charles A. Pillsbury had put up $10,000 for an interest in a Minneapolis flour mill and, as Pillsbury assumed control of the growing company, men arrived from the eastern states to operate the area's gristmills.

Life was hard for the Marses in Newport. The worst happened when Frank contracted polio as a young child. Luckily, he survived the disease—but not before it left its crippling mark. For the rest of his life, Frank could neither stand nor walk without the assistance of a cane.

Yet the origins of the Mars candy empire can be traced to Frank's bout with polio. Frank was too ill to be left in an upstairs bedroom, unattended. Instead, he would be carried down to the kitchen each morning, where his mother could watch him as she did her chores.

## Life Is Like a Box of Chocolates

Frank's most vivid childhood memories were of his mother making candy to help cheer him. As she heated the sugary syrup and painstakingly measured its temperature, Frank picked up first-hand knowledge of candy making, which always seemed magical to him.

If she stirred the bubbling mass too vigorously, crystals would form and spoil the texture; if she didn't stir it enough, it might scorch. Remove it from the heat too soon, and the result would be a runny mess; too late, and the mass would harden on contact with the air into an inedible rock-like substance: only when the elusive "soft ball" mysteriously appeared in the cup of cold water his mother used for testing would the texture of the finished product slide off the teeth like velvet and melt against the palate like cream. And there was still the cooling and beating or pulling and pouring to do just right, or all could still be lost.

The fascination of the candy-making process soaked into Frank's being as the heavenly aroma of simmering chocolate filled his nostrils.

Frank regained his health and entered high school, but he knew he was not capable of a physically demanding job, like the one his father had. This limitation didn't bother him; he had seen his father wearily trudging home each night, coated with white flour and coughing from the dust that he breathed in during his 12-hour workday. Although such labor unions as the Knights of Labor and the American Federation of Labor had begun to improve working conditions for the average worker in response to their exploitation during the Industrial Revolution, conditions were far from ideal. Frank wanted no part of the workingman's life.

## Ethel K.

Shortly after leaving high school, Frank became a candy salesman. A job in sales, he felt, was a definite step above being a laborer. Two months after his nineteenth birthday in 1902, he married Ethel Kissack and established a wholesale candy firm.

Though chocolate candy bars were an English invention of the 1840s, Americans didn't begin eating them in quantity until 1894. That was the year Milton Hershey produced piece milk chocolate. In 1900, he began manufacturing the Hershey's Milk Chocolate bar and, in 1908, the Hershey's Almond bar. Hershey manufactured his chocolate bars in German machinery that he had seen displayed in Chicago one year before, at the World's Columbian Exposition.

Eventually, such ingredients as caramel, nuts and marshmallows were added to chocolate by other candy producers.

The Goo Goo Cluster bar is said to be the first American combination bar, dating to 1912. The Baby Ruth bar was born in 1918.

Frank came in on the ground floor, for candy bars did not rise in popularity until after World War I. During that war, the Army was supplied twenty-pound blocks of chocolate, which it chopped into bar-sized pieces and individually wrapped. Soldiers were rationed these crude candy bars in their meal kits. Hershey's Milk Chocolate was the most popular, and such a standard item in a GI's life that they quickly were bartered for cigarettes and other items. When the war ended, the men were hooked on their daily candy bars. They returned home wanting to continue their candy habit. Sales soared.

But at the beginning of the century, young Frank Mars had to travel far and wide to find interest in the candy he wished to sell. He supplied a chain of five-and-ten cent stores, visiting them more often than his own home. Frank's first son, Forrest E., was born in 1904, fifteen months after his marriage. Still Frank's absences continued, as he obsessively coursed farther and farther abroad in search of the big score.

He also did not send money home to his young family. The evidence for this is solid: Ethel K. divorced Frank in 1910, after eight years of marriage, on the grounds of non-support. She was awarded custody of Forrest, and Frank was ordered to pay $20 each month for child support. Forrest was six years old. After the divorce, he was virtually fatherless, seeing Frank only once every few years.

Soon after Ethel divorced him, Frank's candy distribution business failed. Soon he couldn't meet his child support payments; in desperation, Ethel sent Forrest to North Brattleford in the Saskatchewan province of Canada to live with her parents.

The area was a complete change from the bustling town young Forrest had known. In Canada, he traveled 12 miles to a white brick schoolhouse by horseback each day. Now he was motherless as well as fatherless, living with elderly grandparents in a strange world.

Ethel remained in Minnesota and worked as a sales clerk to eke out a marginal living for herself, and to send money for her son's upkeep.

With his mother living hundreds of miles away in a different country, and his father totally absent from his life, Forrest's early life was bleak.

## Ethel H.

Frank still had a taste for candy, but he'd lost his enthusiasm for selling on the road. Instead, he hearkened back to his mother's kitchen and the sweet smell of successful confectionery. He decided to switch his focus to manufacturing. At this time he also married the second of his wives to be named Ethel, and they moved to the Northwest. The former Ethel Healy became both his wife and his business partner as they concocted candy confections from the kitchen of their Seattle home.

Their business soon failed. Frank was only 28, and this was his second bankruptcy. Since the manufacturing company had been closely tied to the family's finances, Frank's creditors seized the couple's personal belongings, including their house.

Frank and Ethel moved to Tacoma and began another candy company. Tacoma proved a poor choice, because a better-established candy business was nearby.

In 1914, Frank again filed for bankruptcy. (Years later, when Frank's son Forrest looked back on his father's bankruptcy, he minimized the significance of his father's questionable judgment by emphasizing that Frank "was caught in the sugar squeeze when the price of sugar dropped from 22 cents to four cents a pound. He went bankrupt and had to start all over again.")

At 31, Frank had failed three times. Short periods of prosperity were three times followed by financial disaster. Undaunted, Frank remembered only the brief successes and plunged yet again into the candy business.

Trying to escape what Frank felt was the jinx of the Northwest, in 1920 he and Ethel moved back to Minnesota, to his home neighborhood between the Twin Cities. Though this choice might seem to have a certain sentimental appeal, it bespeaks Frank's lack of family feeling. Despite the move, he was still nearly as far removed geographically from his son as when he had lived in Washington state.

## Mars Among the Stars

With $400 that he and Ethel scraped together, Frank started his third candy manufacturing business. It was a modest beginning, with Frank and Ethel living in one room above their small factory. Frank's alarm clock would ring at 3:00 a.m. so that he could melt the ingredients that he then molded into butter cream candies. When Ethel arose a few hours later, she would take Frank's finished candies—and a nickel for trolley car fare—into St. Paul or Minneapolis to sell to variety stores. Their best customer was Woolworth.

Frank was on the wrong side of the adage it takes money to make money. He was so cash poor that he couldn't buy ingredients in bulk. Instead, he bought small supplies of sugar from local candy companies. Frank's reputation preceded him: Even when he needed an inexpensive 100-pound sack of sugar, word went out to accept cash only.

Frank invented a butter cream concoction called the Mar-O-Bar, and named his company after this creation. But local tastes preferred a fluffy nougat bar, made with egg whites and corn syrup, manufactured by another local company. Frank dropped the Mar-O-Bar and set out to imitate the more popular nougat bars.

In 1923, Frank produced a new candy bar that, in an allusion to his celestial last name, he called Milky Way. The conceit was prophetic: with this venture, his star was at last on the rise. The item that turned his luck around only weighed a few ounces. It was a light, fluffy nougat candy bar like other popular confections, with one vital distinction. The other bars had vanilla-flavored fillings. Milky Way's nougat center was chocolate-flavored, topped with caramel and covered with chocolate.

Milky Way was an immediate big hit with consumers. And, compared to other chocolate bars, it was relatively inexpensive to manufacture. Chocolate is a far more costly ingredient than the egg whites or corn syrup that go into nougat. The Hershey's Milk Chocolate bar, for instance, is entirely chocolate; the early Milky Way was only 30 percent chocolate.

Over the years, a tale has been told regarding the creation of the Milky Way. The story goes that one day, Forrest—who, in truth, rarely saw his father—was seated at a counter with Frank, enjoying a milkshake. Forrest is said to have suddenly turned to his father, saying brightly, "Hey, Dad, why not put a milkshake in a candy bar?" This legend is used to illustrate the brilliance and precocity of the young Forrest Mars; however, it never happened. Nougat candy bars had already been established as favorites. Frank's version was merely a high-quality imitation, albeit with a different-flavored center.

The new candy bar was an instant success and red ink turned to black. In one year, sales leapt tenfold, to just under $800,000. Soon the Mar-O-Bar company was able to move into a commercial site and employ 125 people. Two years later, Frank showed a loss of $6,000. Even with a popular new bar, he still hadn't learned to operate at a profit. He needed to recoup and regather, and so he leased his only asset—the recipe for Milky Way—to a another candy company.

Frank changed his company's name to Mars Candies in 1926 and began to look for a larger manufacturing site. Chicago, already a bustling and sophisticated midwestern city, caught his eye and in 1928 he built a new plant in the western suburb of Oak Park. Operations began there the following year. Ethel—with Patricia, their new baby—was eager to try life in a more cosmopolitan area.

Frank bought back the rights to the Milky Way candy bar for $5,000 and began manufacturing it from the Oak Park-Chicago plant.

After so many false starts, Frank finally flourished. His company went from strength to strength. His prosperity was guaranteed in 1930, when he introduced the Snickers bar. Although the first Snickers initially lacked a chocolate coating, that very fact gave it a summer advantage: it was one of the first candy bars that had no chocolate to melt on customer fingers.

With the Milky Way and Snickers bars successfully launched, Frank was over the moon. Although the Depression had hit hard, people could forget their miseries for a few minutes by buying an inexpensive candy bar and sinking their teeth into a caramel and chocolate nougat heaven. By 1930, Mars company had total sales of nearly $25 million and profits of $2.5 million. Mars was now one of the largest makers of candy bars in the country.

Frank soon acquired a taste for luxury. At the height of the Depression, he and Ethel were chauffeured in a $20,000 Duesenberg town car. As a runabout, they used a 16-cylinder Cadillac. He also established two getaway homes: one in Minocqua, Wisconsin that he called Marlands; and a lavish Tennessee showplace, Milky Way Farms Racing Stables. The Tennessee horse farm ran to 2,700 acres and cost Frank $2 million. Marlands was reserved for getaway summer weekends as the Marses fled Chicago's heat. There, beside a small lake, Frank built a log "cabin," measuring 100-by-200 feet, containing every modern feature of its day.

## Frank Sets Standards

It was Frank who established a Mars company tradition: pay the highest wages in the industry. With good pay, however, Frank exacted a high standard of conduct—higher, at least, than that common to workingmen of the day. One worker was hired on the spot because he was enough of a gentleman to know to remove his hat when he entered the personnel office.

Frank was especially demanding about cleanliness. His cane served him as a constant reminder of the damage that germs and bacteria can wreak on the human body. Although sanitation protocols in the 20s were not what we know today, Frank expected his factory to be immaculate. Once, he was on the factory catwalk when he spied a worker picking up a candy bar that had fallen off the assembly line onto the floor. The man had barely started to put it back on the line to be wrapped when he was collared, literally, by Frank, and dragged out of the factory and put out of a job.

Like World War I, the Great Depression had an impact on Candyland. Apple stands, hobo jungles and "Brother, Can You Spare a Dime?" notwithstanding, candy sales for the Mars company quadrupled during the Depression. The Mars candy bars sold for a nickel, which was still affordable even for people who couldn't justify more expensive treats. To this day, the candy industry remains one of the few that is relatively recession-proof.

While executives of other industries were leaping from skyscraper windows in despair, Frank continued to introduce new products, including the new 3 Musketeers Bar, which debuted in 1932. This confection was an overnight hit because of a novel ploy: after you tore off the beige wrapper, you would find three mini bars inside. Initially, the 3 Musketeers Bar consisted of a fluffy vanilla nougat section, a fluffy chocolate nougat section and a strawberry nougat section, all three strips covered with a single chocolate coating. Now, it is one long bar filled with light chocolate nougat. But Frank's original three-bars-in-one kicked off sales and launched this candy bar into the solar system, orbiting near the Milky Way. At the same time, Frank decided to enrobe Snickers with chocolate, and this further increase its popularity.

A proud Frank opened his factory doors to tour groups in the early 30s and thousands viewed the manufacturing plant. Some of his early creations are not familiar to us today: Honey Almond, Thrills and Two Bits. The bar Forever Yours was introduced and advertised as the vanilla Milky Way—its center was vanilla nougat, while its covering was dark chocolate, in contrast to Milky Way's chocolate nougat center with milk chocolate coating.

Forever Yours was Frank's first line extension, a technique that enables a company to play off the popularity of one product by introducing a different product that is merely a variation on the tried-and-true. Frank innovated this modern marketing technique.

## Son of Boss

Forrest, in the meantime, graduated from public high school in Lethbridge, Alberta, where his mother had joined him. Forrest was still not convinced his father's candy business would succeed: after all, many times before he had seen his father's pattern of a good start and a bad ending. Thinking it would be easier to make money in coal than in candy, he enrolled in the School of Mining at the University of California, Berkeley.

Frank's support of Forrest was minimal. He paid his son's tuition, but expected Forrest to pick up his own expenses for room and board. In 1923, Forrest took a part-time job in the university cafeteria and worked out a deal whereby he could keep any money saved by the food service. By ensuring that daily menus reflected current meat supplies, he cut costs. He claims this method let him earn about $100 a week, making him "the richest kid" at Berkeley. Making money interested him more than studying; he dropped out of most of his classes and became a part-time student, focusing on his job.

He worked full-time during college summers. When the campus cafeteria closed for the season, Forrest joined a traveling sales team that promoted Camel cigarettes for Reynolds Tobacco. One day while the team was in Chicago, an overzealous supervisor told him to make sure everyone saw his Camel posters. Forrest took his boss literally and plastered advertisements for the cigarettes over every city sign, wall and surface he encountered. The stunt made the newspapers. Forrest was arrested for defacing property.

Frank bailed him out of jail.

Having cultivated a taste for modern business, Forrest lost his interest in mining. He realized he needed a better education in modern manufacturing techniques than Berkeley could offer. So, in his junior year, he transferred to Yale University, where he enrolled in the Sheffield Scientific School. Mathematics was his best subject; he felt it would help him in his old-fashioned need to "save and make do."

Frank was finally able to support his son and pay the significant sum of his undergraduate tuition. Although the two men had rarely been together, Forrest moved to Chicago after graduating from Yale. Forrest was not a particularly good-looking man; his stocky build, large hooked nose and premature baldness did not add to his appeal. The managers and workers at the Chicago plant noted that Forrest had another unattractive attribute: he was insufferably cocky.

Although he had hardly been the prototype of the doting father, Frank made the classic paternal error of letting his heir start at the top. The Mars son was not taught the business from the bottom up, as is standard in many family companies today. Although Forrest was given no formal title, he took advantage of his familial position to order people to put his untried ideas into effect. Some men referred to Forrest as the SOB: son of boss.

Frank gave Forrest the freedom to roam the company and no specific duties, but when he heard of Forrest's arbitrary commands, he countermanded them. Although Frank was proud of his son's potential, a former associate recalls that "he wasn't about to let him run things." Adding to the father-son tension was Forrest's constant commentary about how he could run the business more successfully than Frank.

The Chicago plant was large enough to manufacture some of the country's most popular candy, but it wasn't big enough for both Frank and Forrest after Forrest, in 1932, demanded a one-third share of the business. Frank had no intention of making his bold son a partner. Ethel H., also, resented Forrest's claim, since she was concerned about the size of the inheritance her own daughter would share.

Frank turned Forrest down.

Even a close-knit father-son relationship would have been strained by this refusal. For a young man who felt he had been abandoned in childhood, an acid test had been failed.

"I told my dad to stick his business up his ass," said Forrest, years later. "I'm leaving," I said.

Frank gave Forrest a start-up sum of $50,000 and told him to start his own business in Europe. He also granted Forrest the foreign rights to Milky Way and other candy bars manufactured by the Mars company, a strategy designed to expand the Mars company outside North America while getting his brash son out of his hair.

Forrest took off, eager to "conquer the whole goddamn world."

## Forrest Abroad

Forrest was a driven man. He still harbored resentment against his father for abandoning him and forcing him and his mother into years of impoverishment. Their arguments on the factory floor in Chicago whetted Forrest's need to prove himself worthy of his father's attention and approval, which he had lacked all his life.

When Forrest started off in Europe, his resentment made him decide to take a different direction from his father's. Just as he had chosen coal mining over manufacturing at college, now—in Europe—he jumped into a Parisian shoe-tree business. On the other hand, Forrest was no fool. Just as he had once realized that he was better suited to candy than coal mining, the failure of his shoe-tree business suggested to him that maybe he ought to make use of that Milky Way candy bar recipe after all.

But before he did that, he was perceptive enough to do a little groundwork. Rather than prematurely leaping into production, Forrest wished to learn what types of candy confections had proven popular to European tastes. He wisely intuited that importing a candy bar that was popular with Americans would not necessarily appeal to consumers in different cultures.

His first attempt at market research involved a rudimentary industrial espionage: he took a job at Nestlé in Switzerland, where the effects of the Depression were causing the burgeoning dairy giant to restructure its international milk and chocolate markets. Unfortunately, Forrest proved not to be adept at foreign languages. Great as the opportunities to learn from Nestlé were, he had a particularly difficult time in a country with three official tongues, and decided to make England his home base.

Because Frank would not allow his unproven son use of the Mars corporate name, Forrest named his first company Food Manufacturers, Ltd. With additional loans from the Chicago company, Forrest next bought a small, dilapidated manufacturing plant in Slough, a drab industrial town outside London. He hired 12 workers.

Forrest manufactured a modified version of his father's best-selling Milky Way bar. Right off, he learned that the English have a sweeter sweet tooth than Americans do. So he altered the bar to conform to English sensibilities by using a standard English milk chocolate, sweeter than an American milk chocolate, to coat his Milky Way.

Forrest also changed the candy's name. What was known in the United States as Milky Way became the Mars bar in Britain. He nearly folded when a heavy rainstorm poured through his plant's leaky roof onto the candy bars awaiting shipment. But he survived this disaster, due only to the immediate popularity of the candy bars. Within one year, Forrest had sold two million candy bars and was employing 100 workers. He found the same success in Britain that his father had found in America.

The new slyly-named Mars became the best-selling candy bar outside the United States.

"Once we got over the initial hurdles," Forrest said years later, "and began to make a profit, we seemed to be moving in the right direction."

But profit was not his only mission. "What you have do is make a good product—not just an acceptable product, but the best you know how."

All of Forrest's actions reflected a singular goal: to make the very best product. Sometimes, he seemed tyrannical in his zeal. There was an incident in Slough, for example, when Forrest stopped by a candy store and noticed that one of the Mars bars was improperly wrapped. He stormed back to the plant, called management into a glass-walled conference room and demanded an inspection of the candy bar cases that were ready for shipment.

He didn't like what he saw. Handfuls of the bars began hitting the glass as astonished employees outside the conference room, peering in at the scene from their desks, saw Forrest hurling Mars bars around the room in anger.

As unpleasant and eccentric as his actions were, they reflected his belief that "if you make a really good product that people want and are willing to pay for, money will come.

"And it is best not to think about how much money you will make."

## Mars Marriage, Redux

Before departing for Europe, Forrest had met Audrey Ruth Meyer, the daughter of A. A. Meyer and Charlotte Nichols Meyer, a prosperous midwestern couple. They married in 1930, after Audrey's graduation from Rosary College. The following year, on August 13, their first child, Forrest Edward Jr., was born in Oak Park, Illinois. A year later the young family left for Europe so Forrest could work in Switzerland and ultimately open his factory in England.

Although Forrest still smarted over his virtual abandonment by his father as a boy, Frank was the only example that he had of fatherhood. Forrest replicated Frank's absenteeism when he left his wife and infant son in England while he studied chocolate techniques in Switzerland at Nestlé. In addition, nearly all of his salary was set aside for the business he was planning.

A few years after moving to Slough, Audrey gave birth in London to their second child, John Franklin, on October 1, 1935. The previously sheltered Audrey was at a loss as to how she was to raise her young boys in the unexpected life of emotional and economic deprivation to which her husband had relegated them.

At one point, Forrest's father-in-law, hearing of his daughter's squalid living conditions, traveled to England to insist that Audrey and the children return with him to the United States. She resisted him, but the dispute exacerbated wounds already smarting from Forrest's psychic and financial neglect. These early marital sores never healed and, along with other grievances of Audrey's, would form scabs that concealed festering resentments. In later years, the scars would affect Forrest in ways he never would have foreseen.

This situation did not, evidently, suggest to Forrest that he might have acted differently. His matter-of-fact attitude about these years was expressed several decades later, when he looked back and said of his early experiences in England, "Nothing worthwhile ever comes easy."

And it truly didn't always come easy for Forrest, especially when he experimented with new products. He manufactured a Milky Way bar that included pineapple; the English quickly let him know that the combination of chocolate malt and pineapple was unappealing. Another bar, So Big, also failed.

Though Forrest concentrated on business at the expense of his family, he studied the English and their sensibilities with devotion. He knew they loved their sweets and he knew they loved their dogs. Forrest bought a company that had only been moderately successful, Petfoods Ltd., and began an education campaign. He wished to teach the British what Americans were already learning: that specially designed nutritional meals were healthier for canines than leftover table scraps. With virtually no competition, Forrest soon dominated the pet food market.

Still, this new prominence did not improve his social skills. Those who worked for Forrest's businesses would try to avoid contact with him. "He could be cruel and demanding," said his chief accountant. Anyone who reported directly to Forrest had to have a thick skin to take his belittlement and tantrums.

Forrest's mood didn't improve when he decided to make quick profits by entering the commodities market trading cocoa. He nearly lost everything he had. But he justified his errors by saying that his ventures had to be big, whether they were successes or failures.

## Planetary Eclipse

Meanwhile, back in America, the Mars constellation was showing signs of dimming. Frank's childhood bout with polio, and his later years of unceasing work, were affecting his health. In late March 1934, he traveled to Johns Hopkins Hospital in Baltimore with Dr. Chauncey Mahrer, his personal physician, to see a specialist about his health. He was immediately hospitalized. Ethel H. was called by Dr. Mahrer and told her husband was grievously ill. She and her daughter, by now a married woman living in Chicago, took the train out to stay at his bedside.

Forrest was in London. Despite ominous telegrams, he remained an ocean apart from his father.

Ten days later, Frank Mars was dead of kidney disease and a heart attack. He was only 50 years old.

In one of the worst years of the Depression, Frank Mars left an estate of $3 million. His obituary in *The New York Times*, called in by his family, repeated the family tale that he was a descendent of the founder of Mars, Pennsylvania.

# Two

# The Business Leader: Forrest E. Mars

Forrest must have thought that his time to shine had finally come. The autocratic old man was gone, and he himself had a burgeoning European business plus the rights to the Mars recipes. All that remained was for him to take over his rightful inheritance.

But there was a stumbling block: Frank's second wife. Ethel H. was a tremendous obstacle to Forrest. When Frank died in 1934, he left some shares of the Mars company to Forrest—but a full half of his company went to Ethel. It was an equitable arrangement, for she had been a true partner during the business's start-up years. She had trudged around town selling candy; she had endured years of living above the store and pinching pennies; she had supported the risky move of relocating to Chicago and expanding the company when many a wife, looking at Frank's history of failure, would have balked.

Forrest, naturally, saw the situation rather differently. To him, taking up the reins of Mars not only was some recompense for the years of neglect, but made eminent business sense—he had experience with the field in general and with the company in particular. It was to be expected that he coveted owning and managing the Mars company himself after his father's death.

But what he saw as an asset—his familiarity with the booming concern—others saw as a liability. Forrest had already alienated many of the Mars executives. Aside from wanting to protect her own and her daughter's interests, Ethel wanted no part of her brash stepson.

However, she also did not have any desire to run the company herself. With Frank gone, she promoted her half brother, William L. "Slip" Kruppenbacher, to the company's presidency. Kruppenbacher had earlier joined Mars, Inc. to work under Frank as one of his first full-time salesmen. Before Frank's death, he had risen to vice president and general manager of the firm.

Ethel, now devoted to a life of play and leisure, concentrated any business acumen she had on her beloved Milky Way Farms Racing Stables near Pulaski, Tennessee. Horse breeding and racing were her main interests. She was a familiar figure at the yearling sales at Saratoga, New York, and consistently paid good prices. Spending $600,000 at Saratoga over a six-year period helped establish her popularity. She usually had as many as 25 yearling thoroughbreds at Milky Way. The result was that her horses raced on tracks from coast to coast. Two of them, Whiskolo and Reaping Reward, finished third in the Kentucky Derby in 1935 and 1937, respectively. Ethel was also the leading money winner of the American turf in 1934 and 1936.

She had once bet on a failed candy salesman to bring her to riches, and she had won. Now she turned that foresight to horse flesh, and, once again, the victory of her horse, Gallahadion, in the 1940 Kentucky Derby brought her the winner's cup. The victory paid 35 to one.

## "I am Not a Tax Dodger"– Ethel H.

Ethel knew there was another advantage, besides winning horse races, to maintaining lavish stables. It could be a canny way to shield assets from Uncle Sam.

It was common, in the 30s, for wealthy figures to incorporate their farms and racing stables in order to save substantial tax payments through deducting individual losses on farm and stable operations. This "incorporated pocketbook" clause was based upon the same general idea of an individual dividing him or herself into more than one taxable entity. This way, a person could avoid taxation of income at the rates prescribed in the higher individual surtax brackets or obtain the benefit of deducting, as a corporation, expenditures not allowed to be deducted by individuals. The U.S. government perceived deductions taken through this incorporated pocketbook clause as amounting to tax avoidance, and was even beginning to view the method as tax evasion.

President Franklin D. Roosevelt, living up to his sobriquet among the rich of "traitor to his class," dwelt at length in a 1937 press conference on the incorporation device. This was a forerunner to his eventual request to Congress for an investigation of these practices.

At the Congressional hearings, Arthur Kent, assistant general counsel of the Justice Department, read a list of prominent figures who were escaping taxes through incorporating personal losses. Among those singled out with Ethel Mars were Jock Hay Whitney, the multi-millionaire whose avocation was horse racing, several members of the Du Pont chemical family and comedian Ed Wynn. Ethel was charged with avoiding $66,000 of taxes over a two-year period through her practice of deducting losses from her Milky Way Farms Racing Stables.

Indeed, a description of Milky Way Farms in those days would hardly have rendered a picture of struggle and loss. Ethel employed more than 100 people on the estate. Her horses were stabled in stalls of polished oak. The fields where her registered Hereford cattle grazed were hand-raked. It took nearly a million dollars a year to support Milky Way Stables, and Ethel duly deducted many of these expenses from her taxes.

Even the Congressional committee members—no strangers, by and large, to luxuries shielded from the accounting demanded of ordinary citizens—were mesmerized by Kent's accounting of Ethel's wealth and how she, and others, had taken advantage of loopholes in the revenue laws. Kent equivocated on whether these declared losses fell within the category of legal avoidance rather than illegal evasion. It was clear, however, that these deductions could not have been taken by Ethel as an individual and were only allowable because she had incorporated.

The Treasury Department was convinced that the device of creating corporations to hold, maintain and operate farms and stables for an individual's pleasure was a "potential menace, capable of profitable use by the taxpayer who owns property requiring large personal expenditures."

Several days after these hearings, Ethel had her say to the media. Ethel denied that she operated her stable of race horses with intent to avoid Federal taxes.

"I am not a tax dodger, never have been and do not intend to be," she said with magnificent aplomb.

The incorporated pocketbook clause was eventually amended and Ethel could no longer deduct her racing expenses from her federal taxes. Despite the scare of being named during a Congressional investigation, she was never charged with income tax evasion, nor were any of the other wealthy names whose tax avoidance practices were detailed in the hearing.

## The Competitor: Chasing Mr. Goodbar

As the Mars candy company grew larger, so did Milton Hershey's chocolate business. Unlike Frank Mars, Hershey enjoyed a long life, which spanned from 1857—before the Civil War—through World War II, to 1945. Although Hershey failed in business several times as a young man, he was a firmly established confectioner by the 1890s, and was owner of Hershey's Lancaster Carmel Company. In 1893, the chocolate manufacturing machinery he saw at the Chicago exposition so enthralled him that he sold his caramel business for a million dollars and built his first chocolate factory in 1900.

Hershey created an industry as he pioneered the mass production of milk chocolate. Not only did his factory engineers devise the modern machinery necessary for huge shipments of chocolate bars, but Hershey understood the importance of controlling raw ingredients.

In 1907, the first Hershey's Kisses were sold and, within four years, the company had sales of $5 million. It also produced cocoa and baking chocolate, as well as the Hershey's Milk Chocolate bar and the Hershey's Milk Chocolate Almond bar. In 1925, the Mr. Goodbar chocolate bar was born, and two years later the company was listed on the New York Stock Exchange.

Milton Hershey, through employment and philanthropy, nearly single-handedly kept the Dairy Township and surrounding communities of Pennsylvania employed throughout the Depression. He purposely planned a "grand building campaign" to expand the area around the Hershey plant so that a maximum number of residents would have employment. A community center, museum, sports arena, stadium, office building, and 150-room luxury resort hotel were built, in a setting of lavishly landscaped parkland mulched with cocoa bean husks and neat streets lit by Kiss-shaped street-lamps. Not only was no one laid off during the Depression, many new jobs were created.

Also benefiting were young boys who were orphaned, or, later, whose families could not take care of them. Because Hershey and his beloved wife Catherine were childless, they established the Hershey Industrial School for orphans, which is now the Milton Hershey School. When Catherine died prematurely in 1915, her husband gifted the school with stock valued at $60 million a few years later. (When Frank Mars died in 1934, no substantial philanthropic gifts were left in his will or made by the Mars heirs.)

After the Depression lifted, Hershey developed a candy bar with crisped rice, called the Krackel bar. Hershey's Miniatures chocolate bars were introduced the following year. Despite Milton Hershey's lack of interest in advertising any of his products directly to the consumer, the company enjoyed tremendous growth based on the popularity of Hershey chocolate. Over the years, the demand for the company's products threatened the other candy bar manufacturers.

## M&M's: Smarter than Smarties

Though thwarted in his ambition to take over his father's company, Forrest Mars continued to build on his success in Europe. By the end of the 30s, he had laid the foundation for two sound businesses. As Hitler began moving westward through the European continent, Forrest took his family—which now included his only daughter, Jacqueline Anne, born in London on October 10, 1939—back to the United States.

He also set up the Audrey Meyer Mars trust on January 3, 1940 for the benefit of his wife. Upon her death, the trust, which was established with a portfolio of publicly traded securities worth at least $800,000, was to be divided among their three children.

Forrest sailed for home, leaving the candy and pet food business in the hands of an English associate. He had done extremely well in England, virtually jump-starting an entire pet food industry and correctly judging what type of candies appealed to English tastes.

Forrest figured that if he could vary the ingredients in American candy bars to appeal British consumers, he also could vary the ingredients in English candies to attract American customers. He returned to America with the rights to make one of Britain's most popular candies in the United States.

Smarties—a small, round, pastel-hued sugar-coated chocolate treat—had been popular in England for several years, having been first produced in 1937 by a giant English candy company, Rowntree and Company, Ltd. In exchange for the rights to Smarties, Forrest traded to Rowntree the English and European rights to Snickers candy bars.

Forrest saw Smarties—that is, an Americanized version of Smarties that he would manufacture—as both a new candy line and also an answer to chocolate companies' worst nightmare, the heat of summer. Forrest remembered Frank's early summer success with Snickers, which initially became popular because it lacked the typical chocolate coating that melted on consumers' fingers.

Before the advent of air-conditioning, retail stores would cut back their stock of chocolate candy during warm weather. Forrest hoped to capitalize on an improved version of Smarties. But the candy coating of Smarties had never been hard-shelled and so Smarties would actually melt in the hand. Forrest sought a more brittle candy shell that would circumvent the chocolate's softening in its packaging during summer months, and would stop the candy from melting in a warm hand.

## Sleeping with the Enemy

Forrest was an admirer of successful modern businessmen and wanted to learn from their lives. He looked up to Milton Hershey, now in his 80s, and he ingratiated himself with Hershey's president, William F. R. Murrie, by traveling to Hershey, Pennsylvania to spend Sunday afternoons with Murrie and his son Bruce.

As the European war threatened the security of the United States, Forrest had another worry. Cocoa supplies would be disrupted by the war. To continue manufacturing candy, Forrest would need to maintain a massive, uninterrupted supply.

Forrest knew that the dwindling cocoa supply would soon be out of reach of a small food producer. He developed a canny—and ethically questionable—strategy. He would befriend Bruce Murrie and eventually make him his minority business partner. Through his friendship with the younger Murrie, Forrest could prevail on him to use his leverage with the giant Hershey company to supply their partnership with enough cocoa to make his new candy. Forrest was careful to retain control of this new venture and talked Murrie into taking only a 20 percent share.

Murrie later said, "We had tremendous help from my father—an assured supply of chocolate and a lot of technical help."

The scheme to make Murrie his partner may have been underhanded but it was clever. And it worked. In 1940, in a plant in Newark, New Jersey the first M&M's rolled off the assembly line. Pellets of chocolate were covered with thin candy shells in a panning process. The candy's initials derived from the names of the company partners, Mars and Murrie, and the company that produced them was called M&M Ltd.

For the first few years, the candy bits themselves did not carry the M imprint (for Mars) that they have today. The colors of the round candies, a little larger than we know them, were similar: brown, yellow, orange, red and green. There was also a violet hue.

Forrest aggressively promoted M&M's Chocolate Candies to the United States military, eager to supply its fighting men with a candy treat that could withstand climate extremes. M&M's were immediately popular with soldiers and sailors overseas and with Americans at home.

Similarly, in England, Forrest's company won a contract to supply Milky Way bars to the fighting forces. Large consignments of the candy bars were furnished to English soldiers.

The only lasting reward for Murrie, who sold his 20-percent shareholding to Forrest in 1949, was to be immortalized as the second "M" in the candy's name. Forty years later, in the mid-80s, an aggravated daughter of Bruce Murrie thought her father had been treated shabbily by Forrest and raised the issue of fair compensation to Mars, Inc.

"His name lives on in each M&M," was the company's terse and conclusive response.

## The Birth of Uncle Ben's

Candy and pet food, two totally different industries, might involve sufficient challenge for most businessmen. They weren't enough for Forrest, however. Although he coveted his father's company, he summed himself up: "I'm not a candy maker. I'm empire-minded."

The self-styled emperor sought another industry, one that was entering a new phase. Rice had been a staple of the human diet for thousands of years but it had always required a lengthy cooking time. The aim of food processing in the twentieth century has been to shorten and simplify cooking in American households, as exemplified by condensed canned soup invented by John Dorrance of the Campbell Soup Company family. Forrest did not have any direct knowledge of rice processing, nor did he nurture a research and development staff who could come up with shortcuts to food preparation. However, word reached him of a new patented technique that had enormous potential.

Forrest sought out the owner of a small rice-processing business in Houston, Texas who had patent rights to produce a quickly cooked, high-nutrition rice using a process called parboiling. In the manufacturers' version of parboiling, rough rice is soaked in warm water under pressure, then steamed and dried before milling. This method of processing rice improves its shelf life while retaining some of its nutritive value. The rice is fluffy and sticks together less than regular milled white rice. Most important, cooking time is reduced.

Forrest formed a partnership with the company owner in 1942, and, again, was careful to retain control of the business. Before long, Forrest convinced his partner to sell out to him.

Forrest petitioned the United States government for assistance in developing what became known as "converted rice." With a government grant, he enlarged his company and formed the nucleus of what is now called Uncle Ben's. The creation of Uncle Ben's Converted Brand Rice was the world's first brand-name raw commodity. The company increased its identifiability and appeal (to white consumers, at any rate) by adorning its packages with the now-familiar kindly—and fictional—black chef.

Forrest began selling rice to the United States Army soon after the opening of Uncle Ben's first production facility. Uncle Ben's rice was an instant hit in households throughout the country.

## Uncle Sam Wants Uncle Ben's

Success carries its own pitfalls. Forrest received a terrible shock in 1944, one that still reverberates throughout the company today. *Reader's Digest* magazine printed a friendly article on the new converted rice, highlighting the success of the Uncle Ben's brand.

The article was so laudatory about the new process that the United States government saw no reason that its military should have to wait to buy Forrest's company's limited supplies of the finished product to feed to its troops. Officials were searching for ways to supply food to soldiers who were stationed in the tropics, near plentiful rice supplies. The federal government made overtures to Forrest to share his patented secrets with other manufacturers, so that several companies could convert rice to feed the maximum number of soldiers, thus helping the war effort.

Forrest saw the government's interest as a dire threat. Luckily, the bureaucratic wheels moved slowly and the war ended before his fears were realized. However, his suspicion of the press, which to many had always seemed irrational, was confirmed. Absolute secrecy, even about the smallest matter, became his strict policy from then on.

## Struggles With Ethel H.

Forrest would never be satisfied with his own accomplishments until he combined his own companies with the Mars candy company that his father had founded. Part of the reason that Forrest was so impatient is that he was sure he would die young, like his father. Of course, Frank had contracted polio as a boy; the disease ruined his health and contributed to an early death. In addition, Forrest's mother, Ethel K., was in her mid-60s and still spry. But logic did not figure in Forrest's desperation to make the Mars company his own.

When Frank died in 1934, he had left only part of the business to Forrest. His widow Ethel H. received the largest amount and retained control of the company, while his daughter, Forrest's half-sister Patricia, received a small share. Company managers also owned minority shares in Mars, Inc.

Neither Forrest's stepmother nor his half-sister worked in the company; Ethel spent most of her time at Milky Way Farms. And Patty, who, unlike Forrest, had been raised in a wealthy household, replicated that lifestyle with her husband James Fleming in the beautiful ocean-front town of La Jolla, California.

The only cloud on Ethel's moneyed life—besides the taxman—was fear of robbery. Given that not unreasonable concern, it would have been wise if she had been less social, or at least had kept her comings and goings out of the society columns. One night in 1940, when the Milky Way Stables house was uninhabited, a burglar cut through a screened window overlooking the porch and made his way up to her second-floor bedroom. He found her hidden money cache, and took about $1,000 in cash. Among the jewelry also stolen was a $10,000 emerald-cut diamond ring, set with ten baguette diamonds in a platinum mounting. Ethel was so well known by this time that her loss, totaled at about $20,000, was reported in the national press.

The media always identified Ethel as the Mars candy manufacturer. In truth, she was rarely at the Chicago plant, but left the running of the company to her half-brother Kruppenbacher, who was now president. The company's growth was slow under Kruppenbacher leadership, for he was cautious and conservative.

Kruppenbacher had introduced new products in the 30s. In 1936, the Mars Toasted Almond bar—roasted almonds on vanilla nougat covered with milk chocolate—had debuted. It is now called the Mars Almond bar. Since Forrest had named the English Milky Way bar the Mars bar, confusion occasionally resulted from the same bar having different names in different countries.

Kruppenbacher also rode the crest of the growing popularity of entertainment on the airwaves (in contrast to Mars's later lack of vision regarding the potential of movie promotion). In 1939, the company sponsored a popular radio quiz show called "Dr. I.Q." The show's hook was that it was not aired from a studio. Instead, the programs were staged in movie houses in cities around the country.

The business subsequently named a candy bar after the show. The Dr. IQ bar consisted of nougat, caramel and peanuts covered with milk chocolate. It was as big a hit as the show, which aired until 1950. Contestants who correctly answered Dr. I.Q.'s questions were given silver dollars, as much as $700 per week. Losers received a box of Dr. I.Q. candy bars.

Another once-popular candy bar that was discontinued was the Ping candy bar. This was a variation on other successful bars. It also had a vanilla nougat center but its chocolate was dark and its nuts were walnuts. A candy bar named Frisco, with almonds and a malted milk nougat, was also produced.

Although the Mars candy company did well during Kruppenbacher's tenure, Forrest resented Ethel H. and her half brother, since he perceived the company as rightfully his. As a minority shareholder, however, he was neither able to control the company nor to put many of his ideas into effect, for Kruppenbacher was—understandably—openly hostile to him. Forrest was stymied in his attempts to persuade Ethel and Patty either to oust Kruppenbacher or to sell their shares to him so he could take charge of the company.

## Ethel H.'s Death

For several years, Ethel H. had been spending winters in La Jolla with her daughter. The southern California climate was more pleasant than either Milky Way Farms in Tennessee, or her Illinois residence in River Forest. In the winter of 1945, she fell ill and was hospitalized near Patricia's home. She died on the day after Christmas, at only 61 years of age.

Now the struggles between Forrest and his father's second family began in earnest. Forrest "was frantic at the notion that anyone except a Mars should control the company," said a close family friend. However, upon Ethel's death, her daughter Patty—who was just as much a Mars as was Forrest—inherited more shares, and Kruppenbacher assumed the chairmanship of Mars.

Forrest still craved control of the Mars company above all. Patty had no interest in it beyond her dividend check, needed for her opulent lifestyle and her large family of seven children. Forrest's strategy was to persuade her that he would make more money for her than Kruppenbacher.

Not only did Forrest fail in his mission but he naturally exacerbated the strain between himself and Kruppenbacher, who, along with other employees, owned nearly one-third of the company. The remainder of the shares belonged to Forrest and Patty.

Forrest now established a beachhead in the heart of enemy territory. In 1946, he used his leverage as a significant shareholder to insist on keeping an office in the Chicago headquarters. That office became the staging arena for an attempted corporate takeover. But espionage is always a danger in covert operations: Kruppenbacher was warned of the nascent coup by loyal managers and he petitioned Patty for her support. Then, rather than confront Forrest directly, Kruppenbacher waited until his adversary was out of town to institute a pass system, without which no one could gain access to the grounds. Forrest, of course, was not there to claim his pass; therefore, when he returned to Chicago, he was barred from entering Mars company property.

Kruppenbacher also set about precluding any attempt at counterespionage among his own ranks. He fired a manager suspected of allegiance to Forrest; Forrest, confirming Kruppenbacher's suspicions, immediately hired the man to work for M&M Ltd.

Meanwhile, Forrest continually wheedled Patty to sell him her shares. In response, Kruppenbacher paid Patty a four-day visit to convince her that she had little in common with a half-brother she rarely saw as she grew up. And Patty remained loyal to Uncle Kruppenbacher, who was so heavily involved in the manufacturing process that "he bled sugar and water," according to an associate.

The following year, when the company had sales of about $30 million, the two men agreed to a truce. Forrest was given control of one-third of the board's nine seats. But under cover of the cease-fire, the younger man further undermined his rival. He used his considerable minority strength to keep the board members at odds with each other as he presented evidence of Kruppenbacher's poor management at board meetings.

This was a family business run amok. Forrest Mars could not control his passion to take control of Mars, Inc., even though many of his actions harmed the very company he so desperately wished to command.

## Marland

Forrest had no desire to move his family back to England after the war. Food rationing was still in effect and the winter weather was particularly bitter. He aspired to the life of a country gentleman, an influence of England and his step-mother's Tennessee stables, and he began to shop for his own farm.

Forrest did not want to be isolated and would not consider buying a farm that was distant from a major city or airport. Since his M&M site was in New Jersey, he wanted to remain on the east coast. A number of his wealthy neighbors in New Jersey spoke of their estates in the Middleburg area of central Virginia. Realizing that the region was only a good hour from Washington, DC and National Airport, Forrest looked into buying a horse farm there.

The Virginia hunt country—an area including towns in Fahquier and Loudon Counties—was developed by New York industrialists who sought more temperate climes for riding and fox hunting, and who were also attracted by the lower prices for large land tracts. Edward H. Harriman, the railroad magnate, brought the Orange County Hunt Club to The Plains in 1903, bypassing Middleburg and Upperville as they didn't have railroad tracks. Andrew Mellon's ex-wife and John Hay Whitney were other early members.

The Orange County Hunt developed rules and regulations—all incomprehensible to non-fox-hunters—that made it as exclusive as England's famous Quorn Hunt. Forrest learned that he could not hunt as a guest unless he had been mounted by a landowner (provided a horse by a member) and had spent the previous night in that member's house. The Hunt made exceptions for no one: in the 20s it refused the Prince of Wales himself permission to hunt, since he had not spent the night in a landowner's house.

Forrest assured his own status by buying an estate, which he named Marland after his father's Wisconsin vacation home, Marlands. He purchased the 740-acre farm, nestled in the Blue Ridge Mountains' foothills, in 1949. Marland was located in the area of The Plains known as Zulla. Because he wanted to oversee the management of his farm actively, and still run his international company, Forrest moved the headquarters of Food Manufacturers to 15th St. N.W., in Washington, D.C. He also kept an office at Marland, employing a secretary, on whom he grew to depend, and working at a polished roll-top desk that he kept neat and free of clutter.

Among Forrest's interests were horse breeding and racing, and he saw these activities as a business as much as a hobby, even though he admitted they were rarely profitable. Perhaps remembering the trouble his stepmother had when she deducted her racing expenses, he justified his hobby: "If it weren't for the write-offs that are made possible under our present tax structure, we would not have the racing sport as we see it today. While the federal government 'loses' about $1,200 on each horse bred for racing, it makes it up by a substantial margin from earnings of winning horses. That's why the IRS encourages the breeding of horses for racing."

The farm was huge. Near its racing compound was the Black Angus cattle ranch, with 300 steers that were raised to a weight of about 900 pounds, then sold to feeders in Pennsylvania who fattened them further and sold them to be butchered into steaks, which were shipped to New York. To attract workers to Marland, Forrest built four concrete-block houses on Zulla Road for his help, whom he treated with more respect than he generally showed his corporate employees.

Once, decades later, actor-producer Robert Wagner was in the area with a cameraman, looking for an estate on which to shoot the television pilot "Line Street" (later scrapped after its teenage star Samantha Smith was killed in a small plane crash). The photographers and cameramen saw Marland and started to photograph the estate for a possible site location. Marland staff flew outside, waving the Hollywood intruders away.

However, the nouveau-riche industrialists of America who had built estates in Middleburg did not fully appreciate the sort of country-squire shabbiness Forrest must have admired among the true English aristocracy. Once, after bird hunting with his dogs, Forrest stopped by a local coffee shop still wearing his old clothes. He realized he had no money on him and asked a neighbor if he would stake him to a cup of coffee. After Forrest left, the coffee shop owner chided Forrest's neighbor, saying that he was encouraging bums to beg coffee!

Marland, however grand, was not sufficient to form a bond for the fragmented family. Audrey Mars was infrequently at Marland, preferring to travel and to stay closer to Washington. For years, Forrest's business travels had kept him away from Audrey and the children. Now their separation was by mutual consent, particularly as Audrey was convinced that Forrest was having an affair with one of his employees. In Audrey's absence, Forrest's secretary at Marland assisted in managing aspects of his personal life that might have otherwise been assumed by his wife.

Their house at Marland, for example, reflected the fashion of the period and the Mars family's rather conventional taste. It was decorated in a post-war vision of colonial America, wedded to a romantic image of an English country house. The living room had overstuffed sofas, with oil paintings of horses and hunting dogs hung on the walls. There was the obligatory grand piano, with photographs of the children and Audrey. The dining room had a long walnut table; there Forrest, like an aging Citizen Kane, often would eat in magnificent isolation, at an island of crystal and porcelain at the far end of the gleaming bare board.

## It's Howdy Doody Time!

In the 50s, Mars was one of the first candy companies to sponsor a television show. The children's program they underwrote, *Howdy Doody*, was to become a cultural icon of that era. The candy bar most prominently advertised on the show was the Mars Coconut Bar.

For his part, having failed to gain control of the candy company his father founded, Forrest concentrated his energies on Food Manufacturers. Within the next decade, it became several times larger than Mars candies, partly due to the conservative management at Mars.

When the war ended, sales of M&M's candies began to slip. An incident exemplifies Forrest's belief in this product, as well as his willingness to treat employees equitably on money issues.

An M&M employee and shareholder was down on his luck. He mentioned to Forrest that he needed to sell his shares in the company. Forrest begged him not to, as the stock was experiencing a temporary setback and was undervalued at the time. When the employee insisted that he had to sell, Forrest overpaid the man, by a factor of five, what his shares were worth on the market.

Forrest was convinced that all he needed was a sound marketing hook to keep the little candies popular. In 1954, the company's advertising agency came up with the answer when it introduced the slogan, "The milk chocolate melts in your mouth—not in your hand." The same year, Forrest extended the M&M's line to include a peanut-centered confection called M&M's Peanut Chocolate Candies.

All of Forrest's enterprises were expanding, in part due to his canny reliance on advertising. Unlike Milton Hershey, Forrest had no compunctions about pushing his products in the marketplace. He was one of the first manufacturers to aim advertising directly at children and he made heavy use of television to get his message to them. Watching his ads dramatically increase sales for M&M's, Forrest realized he could use advertising to his advantage for Uncle Ben's rice as well.

By 1960, Food Manufacturers had sales of $200 million, which represented about $30 million in sales from Uncle Ben's and a staggering $170 million from M&M Ltd. Forrest's company was now four times larger than the Mars candy company in Chicago. Capacity needs required Forrest to construct a plant in Hackettstown, New Jersey in 1958 and, in the early 60s, he extended manufacturing to Europe with a factory at Veghel, in the Netherlands.

But Forrest was not satisfied. He would not be satisfied until he could take control of the candy company he believed to be his birthright.

## Forrest Ascendant

Frank's candy company was not only failing to match the growth of Forrest's business; it was actually declining. Kruppenbacher, by now an elderly man, could no longer head the company, and in 1959 its leadership was assumed by Patty's husband James R. Fleming. Sales went south under Fleming. The change in stewardship did not improve relations between the majority owners and Forrest.

In 1964, the company had sales of $50 million and assets of about $23 million, as compared to Forrest's Food Manufacturer sales of $200 million and assets of $56 million.

Kruppenbacher died soon after his retirement. After Kruppenbacher's death, his family, who had inherited his shares, watched their value decline under Fleming. In 1962, they decided it would be wise to sell their Mars shares—about 15 percent of the total—back to the company. They received $5.5 million. Forrest had managed to pick up a few more shares, so he had about 41 percent of the company, as did Patty. A small coterie of managers, loyal to the Kruppenbachers, owned the remaining 18 percent. The company was unstable and no one was happy.

When Patty became seriously ill in the early 60s, Forrest saw his opportunity. He convinced her to sell her shares. The the year was 1964. Patty received stock that provided a minimum income of $350,000 each year. Her husband was allowed to keep his title and his salary was increased from $100,000 to $125,000.

Employees were paid the sound sum of $1,800 for each share they owned.

Tragically, Patty died the next year, following her long bout with cancer. She was still in her 40s, even younger at her death than her father Frank had been when he died at age 50. Her shares went to her seven children.

Forrest now had what he wanted. He controlled Mars.

# Three

# The Legend: Forrest E. Mars

The poor little rich kid is an icon of American lore, with good reason. Forrest Jr. and John, along with their younger sister Jackie, were raised as upper-class children: they did not always have day-to-day contact with their parents, especially their father, as Forrest and Audrey were engrossed in their own activities.

Audrey usually lived under the same roof as her offspring, but nevertheless her interests took her far afield. She was, for instance, a volunteer for the American Cancer Society, eventually becoming president of the Virginia chapter and chairman of its board. As part of her travels for the cancer association, she established cancer societies in Indonesia, Taiwan and Thailand. Although she was not as much of an outdoorswoman as her husband, she loved animals and was also active in worldwide wildlife groups.

"Audrey was a hard driving, domineering woman," remembered one man who knew her well. "She had more of an interest in the outside world than her husband and was a significant force behind the National Symphony Orchestra of Washington, D.C."

Forrest came into town only at Audrey's command. "She would hardly give him the time of day except when she wanted him to do something. She would order him to come back here to go to the Symphony Ball. He would come back, put in an appearance and then leave town again."

Although Forrest would appear at these social events, he eschewed walking through the front door like everyone else, for fear of photographers. Instead he would enter a building through the service door and come into the ballroom through the kitchen.

As for Forrest's own activities, he was often traveling on business or working long hours at the Washington headquarters. Even when at home, he didn't allot much time to his children. He found the workings of Marland more engrossing than his progeny, and kept a more watchful eye on the operations of his estate than on the development of the next generation.

Fox hunting, the sport of kings, continued to be a favored pastime. Forrest was active in the Orange County Hunt. But in the early 60s he fell when his horse, in Audrey's words, "slithered and slipped" on the approach to a jump. He was hospitalized after suffering head injuries and spent the weekend at the Fahquier county hospital. (Also riding in the hunt that day was Jackie Kennedy, the president's wife, who had rented the Glen Ora estate several miles from Marland and who had witnessed his fall.)

Audrey, who did not share her husband's passion for Marland, led the busy social life of a clubwoman and volunteer. She traveled nearly as much as he. Not with him, though: Audrey and Forrest lived separately for most of their marriage.

So the children were, to a large degree, left to their own devices and the ministrations of hirelings. It was an odd upbringing, even for upper-class children who do not usually interact with their parents as often as middle-class children do. Both boys, Forrest Jr. (nicknamed Forrie) and John, were sent to Hotchkiss preparatory school and then to Yale University. Daughter Jackie graduated from Miss Hall's School in Pittsfield, Massachusetts and "came out" wearing a pale pink organdy ballgown at the Middleburg Community Center with other debutantes in 1957. The following year, she was presented to Queen Elizabeth at Buckingham Palace. In 1961, she graduated from Bryn Mawr College with a degree in anthropology.

While still teenagers, the children were given chores and their father made it clear that, as adults, they would have to work for whatever they received. They were raised as Episcopalians, which was a compromise choice made by Audrey, and Forrest, whose family had been associated, it is said, with the Society of Friends (Quakers).

It was expected that the boys would have careers in Forrest's businesses. John, who is better at figures than at writing, majored in industrial engineering at Yale because it did not require a thesis. After graduating in 1957, he served in the Army for two years—at a time when the only war engaging America was the Cold one.

Forrest Jr. did not benefit from such fortuitous timing. He graduated from Yale in 1953, with a major in economics. The Korean conflict was winding down when a notice arrived at Marland. It ordered Forrie to report to the local courthouse for induction into the U.S. Army.

## "We Feed [M&M's] to Our Hogs"— Forrest Jr.

The armed services are renowned for the leveling acculturation effect it has on its draftees. It would take more than the U.S. Army, though, to socialize a Mars.

Two other local young men, John Gott and John Wayland, had also received induction notices. It was a cold, wet October day when they arrived at the Fahquier county courthouse shortly before 7:00 a.m. to await the bus that would take them to Alexandria, Virginia to be sworn in.

John Gott remembers, "We were standing there trying to keep warm when up pulls a limousine, probably the first one I had ever seen. A liveried chauffeur got out, carrying a little black leather satchel that he placed on the courthouse steps. Then he opened the door for a pudgy looking young man, with yellow-red hair. The driver tipped his cap and drove away.

"The overweight man walked up the steps and asked if we were waiting for the bus to be inducted. Soon after, Mrs. Lucille Scates, the draft board clerk, arrived with three tickets. She called out, 'John Gott, John Wayland, Forrest Mars Jr.'

"That was the first we knew who this man was, although we were aware of the Mars family. We wondered what Forrest Mars Jr. was doing with us country boys being inducted into the Army."

After their induction at Alexandria, the three men were sent to Ft. Jackson, North Carolina, where they posed with each other for pictures in the unusually warm weather. Returning to the tent that housed them, they started talking to a southern recruit who was relaxing by his bunk, eating candy.

Gott says, "Suddenly, this man remembered his manners and said, 'Would you like to have some M&M's?'

"I started to take some candy when Forrest Mars turned around and turned up his nose with the greatest air of superiority.

"'We feed those to our hogs,' Forrest said smugly."

Gott continues, "I'll never forget the look on the face of that boy who'd offered him the M&M's."

## Forrest Grump

Forrest Jr. wasn't long for the life of an ordinary recruit. On the second day at Fort Jackson, Gott and Wayland went back to their tent and found that Forrest had gone. He had made good on his word that he would not have to go through basic training with the rest of the men. He boasted that he was going to business school at Ft. Benjamin Harrison in Indiana, instead.

"He did not go through basic training for eight horrendous weeks with us poor country boys," remembers Gott. "He was spared that."

"We said to each other, 'Well, this is what money does for you.' It left a real bad taste in our mouths."

After mustering out of the Army's business school, Forrest Jr. went to Manhattan to serve several years at Price Waterhouse, the accounting firm that handled his father's business accounts. He left Price Waterhouse to join his father in 1960, four years before the elder Forrest gained control of the Chicago company. Managers at the various family businesses throughout the world dreaded to hear that Forrest Jr. or his younger brother John were to be assigned to their operation. Some of their feelings were not based on the brothers' characters but merely reflected resentment at being stuck with the boss's kids and the unwelcome attention this would bring from Forrest Sr.

Forrest treated his sons worse than he treated any other associates, yelling at them, haranguing them and screaming so loudly that he could be heard in the next room. The associates felt sympathy for the young Mars men and were embarrassed at being forced to witness their humiliation.

It was therefore a relief to all when, because the company needed someone to plan the opening of a new headquarters office, Forrest Sr. put his older son in charge, removing him from any possibility of being involved with line responsibilities. But the following year, Forrest Jr. was sent to Veghel, in the Netherlands, where his father desired to start a manufacturing plant.

It wasn't unusual for a factory to have a fence, especially a factory that was associated with a business as proprietary as Forrest Mars's. However, when Forrest Sr. arrived for the Veghel plant's opening, he grew enraged when he saw a flimsy fence that he thought was an unnecessary expense. In front of all eyes, he kicked it down.

Later, a factory fire at the same plant maddened the elder Forrest. He demanded profuse apologies from Forrest Jr., who headed the Veghel site but could not, logically, be blamed for the fire.

Speaking of Forrest's treatment of his sons, one associate remembers, "He was terrible to them."

## Forrest Takes It to the Top

In 1964, few of the staff at the Mars, Inc. headquarters in Chicago had met Forrest Sr., although some of them had heard the tales about how he treated his sons. Most of the Mars staff knew his own father Frank had sent him to England as a young man, where he had established his own successful candy and pet food companies. But his work there plus the demands of his United States businesses, M&M and Uncle Ben's rice, meant that his visits to the Chicago plant were infrequent.

In addition, the elder Forrest's penchant for privacy meant that he declined attending any trade convention or industry activity. He had never spoken to the press and never given an interview. In fact, hardly an employee knew what he looked like, as he had never allowed his picture to be taken. His avoidance of photographers amounted to a fetish.

Mars employees who were wise did not refer to the protracted periods of hostility between management and Forrest. After all, Forrest had won the final battle and was now in charge of Mars. Managers were all too aware that sales had been slipping and they were more than a little anxious about their first meeting with the new owner.

Forrest strode into the beige conference room where he had gathered the top Mars staff. The overhead lights reflected off his nearly bald head. The narrow ring of hair that he still possessed was gray; after all, Forrest E. Mars Sr. was 60 years old. But despite his age, he reminded some of the men of a bantam rooster: quick and aggressive, despite his squat stature. He dressed in the English style, wearing a wide-labeled, double breasted suit of the type that was rarely seen in a midwestern city 30 years ago.

"We didn't know if he was ahead of the times, or behind," commented one executive.

Forrest began with the expected introductory comments and a few jokes that were met with dutiful chuckles by his audience. He talked of the merger between his 30-year-old company Food Manufacturers (which by now had dropped the English "Ltd." in favor of the American "Inc.") and the business Frank Mars had founded. The companies were to be united as Mars, Inc. He notified the group that the Chicago company was to be known as the Mars Candies Division. (Later, the candy unit became M&M/MARS.)

Then came the zinger.

"I'm a religious man," he told his managers. They remained silent, not sure where his remark was going. The image of a religious man accorded ill with the irascible, ruthless personality they had heard of.

Suddenly, Forrest slipped from his chair at the head of the conference table and disappeared from sight. Had he dropped his pencil?

His shiny scalp popped up above the table top and the men saw Forrest close his eyes. "I pray for Milky Way, I pray for Snickers, . . . "

The managers were astounded and unnerved by this introduction to their new owner.

## The Faces of Forrest E. Mars Sr.

Forrest was an intense businessman behind the scenes, but an owner who was infrequently seen in any of his worldwide operations. He said that he gave his division presidents and managers complete authority and responsibility for their operations. In fact, Forrest only saw them a few times a year, usually at board meetings.

Although he was rarely in attendance, he made his presence felt. He had six managers who were liaisons for the division presidents on Forrest's behalf and would report back to him on whether or not the division presidents were meeting the goals Forrest had defined for them.

Along with paying top salaries, Forrest talked a good line of being as supportive of managers as possible. "We give them every opportunity to make it," he said in his only interview, given in 1966 to a trade journal. "Give them all the help they need. And, of course, full authority and responsibility.

"No one wants to see anyone fail. One of the greatest satisfactions is to see a person succeed—to accomplish what he sets out to do."

Although few could argue with such lofty pronouncements, in practice he strayed from his benign theory. Managers were willed to succeed—but only if they used the methods Forrest had detailed in his many operating plans. Executives and workers alike had to be united in a coordinated effort to make the best product for a sound profit . . . Forrest's way.

Forrest used his engineering background as rationale for his theories of "scientific management," which he kept up-to-date by extensive reading of top management theorists of the day. An unusually high proportion of top staff had graduate degrees in engineering or business. "What Forrest likes is brains," commented his former partner, Bruce Murrie.

Meticulous flow charts, tables and graphics illustrating the path to profits were disseminated to managers from the shadowy power off-stage. Top executives were also sent reading lists with such titles as *General and Industrial Management.*

Manuals explaining flow of operations and authority were written and distributed to all employees. Few employees ever actually saw Forrest, but they knew what he expected them to do. Efficiency of scale was a key concept for the growing company. Many controls were in place and Forrest checked on a division's statistics frequently. Along with controls, incentives were given. While there were few questions about who was ultimately in charge, operations controls were more decentralized than was common for the time.

Although the company's principal goal was growth in sales, Forrest's most important performance measure was return on total assets used in the business. Applying a complicated formula, he demanded both a seven percent annual growth from all divisions *and* a 22 percent return on investments.

Oddly, if a division head reached higher percentages than the seven percent growth and 22 percent investment return

Forrest sought, the manager would be closely questioned and, rather than receive praise, he would be criticized. Forrest didn't want to see any deviation from his formula; he figured that anyone making a greater return was not spending enough on product improvements or advertising.

Forrest also made sure that Mars, Inc. was the first confectionery company to adopt new technologies. Besides demanding high standards for quality and cleanliness, he automated production lines earlier than his competitors. On the other hand, he eschewed practices he considered unproductive, no matter how widely they were followed by other industry giants. So for years, the company would not produce holiday candy, as Forrest felt special runs were an inefficient use of manufacturing facilities.

Forrest did want to learn from others where they established systems he admired, and he patterned his own reporting system after the Du Pont corporation's. Each division leader had to produce detailed performance charts, showing actual and projected production, and defend them to Forrest at regular intervals. "Profit is our single objective," was his leitmotif. Forrest forbade his managers to bring aides with them to these meetings: they were on their own as they faced him.

On top of this rigorous fine-tuning, Forrest always held the trump card where staff were concerned. When a manager was hired, he was asked to sign a letter of resignation to be used if he didn't meet his goals within three years.

## Down-to-Earth Mars

Taking over his father's company constituted more than donning a discarded cloak of leadership and continuing business-as-usual for the new owner. It was a chance to adapt the firm to his own style. The Mars company began to change immediately upon Forrest Sr.'s assuming Frank's mantle. He took a successful but conventionally run confectionery firm and shaped it to his personality. Many of the practices and principles Forrest put into operation are still the ones that guide the corporation today.

The first of his changes was a democratization of the company, several decades before other business theorists preached its wisdom. Symbolic reminders of the old regime were dismantled as Mars candies grew to look more like the M&M and Uncle Ben companies. Although Forrest himself was autocratic, he could not abide seeing this characteristic in his managers. In Forrest's mind, they were no better, and no less important, than the lowest-level employee.

Forrest's edicts changed the familiar Mars landscape: for example, there were to be no more reserved parking spaces for executives. The company's helicopter was sold. The executive dining room that resembled a men's club, with stained glass windows and family crests, was torn out and its oak walls stripped. Soon, all workers were eating in the same cafeteria.

Private offices disappeared, too. In their place appeared small work areas. The rare individual who retained his own office room now had little privacy, with wide glass windows installed in place of walls. Closed doors were barriers to communication, said Forrest, and glass walls stimulated the open flow of ideas.

The shortage of privacy was also exemplified by the two-way mirrors that Forrest installed.

Although the company, over the years, has maintained its payroll at about 10 percent above the industry average, Forrest actually raised salaries about 30 percent when he first took over Frank's company. Forrest always thought paying higher-than-usual salaries a wise practice that helps avoid unionization. Employees, including managers, can earn an extra 10 percent of salary for each day on which the employee is punctual. This policy led one worker to comment, "I used to think it was a wonder no one got killed rushing to work."

In addition, bonuses were linked to rises in sales. These bonuses could amount to as much as 15 weeks' salary. The down side: when sales drop, so do salaries.

Employees are termed "associates" and few of them have titles. Salaried employees are differentiated by zones, which have steps within them. Zone 6, made up of the sales staff and factory foremen, is at the bottom of the hierarchal pyramid while Zone 1, which then consisted of Forrest Sr., in solitary splendor, is at the top. The division managers are lumped together in Zone 2, although their pay differs according to sales volume and other factors—especially that division's return on assets. As with sales, if the return falls below the target goal, salaries drop in tandem.

Something else that hasn't changed since those days is the grueling schedule. A 12- or 14-hour day was typical for Forrest Sr.'s top associates; associates are still expected to work long hours.

Forrest's desire for profits, however, were never to come at the expense of the product. As a former employee noted, "When Mars finds a way to make the product better, even if it's more expensive for them, they do it."

Little expense was spared in obtaining the best ingredients. Forrest grew dissatisfied with the company's reliance on chocolate suppliers, even though he found no fault in the quality of the chocolate he received from Hershey Foods and Baker's chocolate. Rather, it simply galled him to rely on other confectionery companies for his products' ingredients. He also figured that manufacturing his own chocolate would lead to improved efficiency of scale.

Packaging, a growing expense with companies who vied with each other in lavish, eye-catching presentation, at Mars was supposed to be held to the lowest possible cost consistent with protecting the candy. "They don't eat the package," Forrest would say. When Forrest found out that his sons were producing a new M&M's product whose container cost 15 percent of the product's retail cost, rather than the 6 percent Forrest thought was ideal, he insisted that the container be scrapped, even though the product was a strong seller.

Everything had to be perfect for Forrest to be content, whether it was the best ingredients or a state-of-the-art manufacturing process. At the Hackettstown M&M plant, for example, any little candy missing part of the M imprint would be rejected. In fact, the imperfect candy was sent down to Marland to be fed to the hogs—just as Forrie had boasted to his boot camp bunkmates.

Cleanliness, as always, remained Forrest's obsession. The Mars manufacturing sites looked immaculate and were constantly measured for bacteria, including the plant floors. If anyone suspected a sanitary problem, Forrest preferred to destroy an entire batch of candy than take a chance with his product.

Advertising for Mars candies was revved up as the budget media time more than doubled. Forrest had used advertising to make M&M's and Uncle Ben's rice into market leaders, and he applied these techniques to his new candies division. He was spending about $30 million in advertising, more than any of his rivals in the candy industry.

## "Be Thankful to God"— Forrest Sr.

Despite his constant criticism and humiliation of his sons, Forrest Sr. continued to promote them. Forrest Jr. was eventually named president of Mars Chocoladefabriek, N.V., which made candy at the Netherlands plant for sale throughout Europe. In the late 60s, he went to Paris to start a new candy venture.

Obviously, Forrest Sr. felt that learning a business overseas as he had done was character forming, for he also sent John abroad, to London to head up the vending machine operation. Following his London experience, John was directed to study Canadian and Australian opportunities for the company and eventually to set up a pet food company in Australia.

Even as Forrest was gauging his sons as successors with a critical eye, he was still creating innovations that would become standards in the confectionery industry. For example, Mars, Inc. was the first candy company to date its products and, similarly, was the first to remove unsold candy after several months. Most companies did not have the sales volume that Mars did and so they could not follow suit. "This [practice] is very risky unless you have Mars' turnover," noted one competitor.

Mars's edge here led to a cycle of growth. Although the average consumer may not have realized that the Mars candy bars stood a good chance of being the freshest on the shelf, retailers preferred Mars products because they knew they would always be in good condition. As a result, retailers gave Mars greater shelf space in their stores. Since candy is an impulse buy, whatever candy bar the hungry consumer sees in front of her is what she will most likely purchase. Mars benefited tremendously from its "facings."

But Forrest kept as close an eye on his sons as he did on shelf space. Wherever the brothers went, Forrest's criticism followed them. He was not hesitant to call them "dumb" and "stupid" in front of others and would fly into a rage if he thought they had made a poor decision.

The young men were also subject to bizarre and arbitrary orders. Once John had the misfortune of accompanying his father to a meeting with the company that had the Mars advertising contract in West Germany. Forrest pointed to the president of the firm and said to John, "We should be thankful to God that we have all these people thinking about our business."

John saw no reason to disagree. "Yes, Father," was his humble response.

Forrest was apparently a man who advocated prayer. "John, get down on your knees and pray."

Which is what John did, never looking up until the meeting ended and his father called him to leave.

No wonder that visits from the unpredictable Forrest Sr. were fraught with anxiety for everyone in attendance.

## An Empire, Not a Dynasty

To the eye of the beholder, the big picture at Mars seemed clear. Here was a man who had taken over his father's business, and who had established his sons in prominent positions in that same business. Succession was assured, it would appear, and the heirs apparent in place to continue the line into the future—descendants in an ever-receding perspective could be expected to maintain the Mars family orbit.

The prescient beholder would have been wrong.

Forrest Sr. was open about his wish to establish an empire, but contrary to popular assumption, he was never interested in founding a dynasty. He wanted the stimulation and challenge of a demanding business, and he needed to see how far he could take the company that his father had founded. Unlike many men who build businesses and say that their greatest hope is to see their sons in the company,

Forrest Sr. had no particular interest in building toward his posterity's future ownership.

In fact, he liked to toy with the idea of giving the whole business up. Most family business owners who do not need capitalization for growth abhor the idea of going public. Not Forrest. In 1966, in his sole media interview, Forrest discussed the possibility of Mars, Inc. becoming a public company.

"Who can tell?" he said. "There is no need for it today." He elaborated, saying that as the company grew in whatever direction the times and needs dictated, he might make that decision.

"Look how Hershey has changed over the years" since becoming a public company, he noted. "If Mr. Hershey were alive today he would be amazed at what is taking place. His company is public, it has grown considerably, it is moving in different directions, and more and more it is being managed by professional managers.

"If there is a need for it, we might do it."

These words stuck fear in his sons' hearts. They dreaded the prospect of Mars becoming a public company, which would make them accountable to outside shareholders. Forrest Jr. and John wanted the same authority their father had: the last word on any decision.

They patterned their own behavior on their father's. Just as Forrest had embarrassed and countermanded them, they would turn on professional managers as the mood struck, becoming irrationally critical and overbearing.

At his post in the Netherlands, Forrest Jr. was furious when he heard a complaint about body odor among the local workers. He had all hands summoned to the cafeteria where he hopped up onto a table and berated them: "You filthy Dutchmen! You must all take a shower." As they left the lecture, each worker was handed a towel and bar of soap — and off to the showers they went.

Anger and criticism were not the only traits the brothers had picked up from their father. Forrest used divide-and-conquer techniques with his sons, which served to make them compete with each other, even though they were usually separated by thousands of miles. Because Forrest belittled his sons constantly, they would curry favor with him at the expense of each other. Thus the father set up a pattern of brother working against brother that continues to this day.

Whatever Forrest Jr. accomplished in the Netherlands was compared to what John had done in London. Often, John fared better in these contests; he was definitely more hard working and aggressive than his older brother and most people—including his father—felt that John was brighter than Forrest Jr.

He was bright enough, at any rate, to be aware of his image in the company. On one factory tour, John was warned to move away from the overhead conveyer. John joked, "In some plants I've been in, they'd have shoved me under."

The guide rejoined, "Maybe they know you better than we do."

## Kal Kan

Forrest's pet food company, headquartered in England, had become the largest dog food packer in the world, with operations in Europe, South America and Australia. The profit margin is higher for dog food than for candy, so naturally Forrest wanted to expand his dog food empire to the United States. To do this, he bought Kal Kan Foods, Inc. in 1968. Kal Kan had been founded thirty years earlier, and, similar to Forrest's M&M's and Uncle Ben's rice products, surged upward in sales during World War II when it supplied the army with food for military dogs. The company also bought the Puppy Palace chain of pet stores but sold it after a few years.

Forrest Sr. immediately expanded Kal Kan, adding two plants in the midwest and moving into new midwestern and eastern markets. By now it had become Forrest's corporate practice to focus on big brand names—like Uncle Ben's and soon, Kal Kan—rather than creating different lines for different distribution channels. Forrest's support of this practice was based on his belief that keeping major brands would create fewer trade conflicts and less fragmentation of brands in the long run.

"Forrest Mars," said one of his executives, "has a powerful entrepreneurial sense. He's good at selecting a proven idea in one part of the world, or from one company, and putting it into operation in another."

Canny Forrest knew that he could always use byproducts from one of his businesses for another. Pet food often uses rice, rather than less extensively available grains, as a filler because of its desirable nutritional attributes. Thus broken rice—a by-product of milling—and small amounts of rice flour could be shipped to dog food plants for further economies of scale.

In England, Forrest Sr. had founded Mars Electronics International (MEI) in 1965. Two years later, he brought the company to the United States. MEI was responsible for the first electronic vending machines, which replaced those that were mechanically operated.

Forrest was interested in any business that he could purchase without debt and from which he could obtain a high profit percentage. He would frequently repeat his old pronouncement, "I'm not a candy maker. I'm empire-minded."

## Crunching Hershey

Although some candy bars were still priced at a nickel, by 1968 they were raised to a dime. But the Woodstock generation, still young and slim, kept buying . . . for the moment. In the early 70s, the pinnacle of Forrest's achievements came when Mars, Inc. passed Hershey Foods Corp. to take the number one spot in the United States candy market. Mars finally outmarketed Hershey. Forrest's acumen recognized the role advertising plays in the consumer's selection of candy and he heavily promoted his blockbusters, Snickers and M&M's.

Forrest was fortunate that his greatest rival was in the hands of a sleepy management. From the beginning of the century until 1970, Hershey had refused to advertise. Founder Milton Hershey believed that a good product sold itself, although he did have the words "Hershey's Cocoa" printed on his car (a 1900 Riker Electric—the first automobile ever seen in Lancaster County).

Hershey Foods did still maintain its strong position in the chocolate market as a chocolate producer. But management was not aggressive, allegedly due to nearly half the company's stock and most of its voting stock being owned by the Milton Hershey School, which was content with its conservative earnings and did not concern itself with management.

Unlike the secretive Mars company, Hershey opened its factory to tourists and had established a visitors' bureau as early as 1915. By the early 1970s, one million people were visiting the plant annually. However, word of mouth could not keep Hershey in the top spot, especially as weight- and health-conscious consumers began to decrease their candy consumption. The company realized that they had to change strategy and began advertising as a defensive measure against Mars, Inc. and other candy companies.

On July 19, 1970 a full-page advertisement for Hershey's Syrup appeared in 114 newspapers. Before the end of the year, advertisements for Hershey products were appearing on radio and television, too. The company also worked a deal with the large English confectioner Rowntree Mackintosh to become the American distributor of Kit Kat Wafer Bar and Rolo Caramels.

By this time, six years after Forrest Sr. had taken over his father's company, Mars products had pulled well ahead of Hershey. Mars, Inc. produced half of the nation's top ten candy bars, and the number one candy of the decade was Snickers.

Through Forrest's marketing strategies, management techniques and blue-sky vision, he had captured the lead position in the candy industry.

Only one question remained.

Could his sons Forrest Jr. and John keep Mars as successful and make it grow more profitable?

## Forrest Mars' Day Off

Both brothers had married by this time, as had sister Jackie. Forrie wed Virginia Mae Cretella, whose father was Albert W. Cretella, a U.S. Representative from the New Haven area, and a Yale graduate. John married Adrienne Bevis, and Jackie married David Badger, a Yale graduate like her father and brothers who similarly followed suit by working at Mars, Inc. None of the wives had jobs; instead, they all began having children soon after their marriages.

In 1973, Forrest Sr. decided that the time had come for him to retire. When Forrest finally let go, he did so completely. He not only retired but he gave the company—at this time, it had sales of $500 million and was virtually debt-free—in equal shares to his three children.

Forrest Jr. and John were named co-presidents. Just as their father had separated them by putting them in different foreign operations in their early years, now he decided that Forrie should head up the well-known candy operations, while John should control the rest of the business: pet food, rice and the vending operations. Both brothers, along with Jackie, were board directors of the company.

The patriarch's departure was astounding. Most entrepreneurial men find it nearly impossible to leave their companies, hanging on well past retirement age and making everyone miserable in the meantime. Forrest Sr., however, was looking forward to the next phase of his life. He remembered how long he had fought his own father for control of the Chicago company, and how he had been 60 years old before it was his. He wanted to hand the whole business over to his children and let them have a chance to run it. He structured his gift through trusts, which helped protect the company from estate taxes and from any irrational acts of his children—such as selling shares outside the family.

Forrest E. Mars Sr. had built an impressive empire. Mars was the largest candy maker in the United States, with sales amounting to about $200 million, and an extra $55 million in the United Kingdom. The Mars businesses, altogether, had sales of one-half a billion dollars.

But as it turned out, Forrest was not yet ready for retirement. Like a modern-day King Lear, he was only going out onto the heath for a while before taking the stage again to goad his offspring.

## The Red M&M's Scare

In 1976, M&M's eaters throughout the nation were surprised, vexed and disappointed when Mars announced it was dropping red-colored candies. The news followed a study conducted by the Toxicology Advisory Committee of the United States Food and Drug Administration that found a statistically significant number of malignant neoplasms in rats that had eaten large quantities of amaranth, or Red Dye No. 2, for 131 months. As a result, the FDA removed the dye from its list of colors approved for use.

This statement should have had no effect on Mars candies. After all, their M&M's were colored red with Red Dyes Nos. 3 and 40, which were not implicated in any studies. But Mars ceased production of red M&M's "to avoid any consumer confusion and concern."

The decision was unpopular with consumers, and sales dipped. M&M's' customers were also confused. If M&M's did not contain Red Dye No. 2, then why stop their production? And, even if they had contained this newly suspect red dye, did that make them crimson pellets of death?

If consumers were unhappy, so were Mars market researchers. After all, focus group studies had led the company to fill 20 percent of each bag of plain M&M's with red ones.

(As well as the red candies, the bag's ideal mix includes 30 percent brown, 20 percent yellow, and 10 percent each orange, green and tan. Peanut M&M's have a different color combination. They are 30 percent brown, 20 percent red, yellow and green, and 10 percent orange. Peanut M&M's are never colored tan, for reasons that the company—of course—refuses to divulge.)

People do become irrationally devoted to their favorite color of M&M. Several syndicated cartoon strips, including *Sally Forth*, have devoted story lines to the 1995 bombshell:

should a new color be added, and if so should it be blue, pink or purple? The company ran a voter poll in 1995 to make its decision; it announced in late March of that year that the newest shade for M&M's is . . .blue. More than ten million votes were cast and more than half the voters chose blue. The first runner-up was purple and, next, pink. Blue M&M's will replace the tan color and will presumably account for 10 percent of the candies. The company highlighted this new color choice by lighting the Empire State Building in blue during the press ceremony held within.

More may depend on M&M's' hues than the casual muncher might think. Members of Van Halen, the rock group, had language inserted in their arena contracts that M&M's were to be included in dressing rooms before each concert... but with the brown ones removed. Once, someone forgot to pick out the browns. The group became agitated at the sight of the brown M&M's and in retaliation wrecked their dressing rooms and the stage.

Most M&M's fans reacted a little more calmly to the Red Scare. They took constructive action by writing to the company or, in the case of one college student, by forming The Society for the Restoration and Preservation of Red M&M's. The University of Tennessee student who founded this society devoted himself to organizing letter-writing campaigns and giving media interviews.

Later, he explained, "There wasn't that much to do at college."

Luckily, Mars assigned a higher priority to the need for red M&M's and reinstituted them in their Christmas holiday package. After all, they could hardly offer green M&M's without the seasonal red.

But following the holidays, consumers realized that the regular brown bags of M&M's Plain and Peanut still lacked the coveted red candies. The post-holiday letdown was worse than usual that year: the company was producing 100 million M&M's each day and not one was red. Mars' action raised further questions: if it was not confusing to use red M&M's at Christmas, then why not continue them year-round?

Only after studying the issue for eleven years did the company relent and, to the delight of their customers, once again begin manufacturing red M&M's.

Why?

Mars, again, refused to comment.

## Ethel M Chocolates

Soon after cutting his ties to Mars, Inc., Forrest Sr. became bored. He and Audrey were not companions in any sense of the word. In fact, she resided permanently at the famed Watergate apartment house in Washington's Foggy Bottom neighborhood. Audrey's apartment at the Watergate was something to behold. She had a duplex that included the apartment next door, which she merged with her own.

"She had a mansion up there," remembered another friend. "Her garden was so large that she had a full-time gardener, a helper and two or three other staff in the Watergate residence. Her garden in this apartment house would have done justice to any estate in Washington." There she became friends with Frankie Welch of Frankie Welch Interiors, the well-known specialist in home interiors and scarf designs whose company is located in Alexandria, Virginia. The ladies would lunch outdoors on spring and summer days, with Audrey dressed always in a designer frock of simple but stunning design.

For his part, although Forrest enjoyed having greater time to hunt and ride, he missed the challenge of operating a business. He felt left out of the action, for example, when the industry doubled candy bar prices from a dime to twenty cents in 1976.

He still found occasion to comment on other developments. He applauded his sons, for instance, when they recognized that most candy bars are bought on impulse and made Mars the first company to place candy displays near retail cash registers.

That's not to say that he didn't also pick up on the negative: if he spotted a poor candy display or picked up a Mars bar that he thought might have been fresher, they got a phone call. "The old man was in still in control in spirit and by telephone," said one associate of the late 70s.

It wasn't enough, though, to keep this 77-year-old man fully occupied. "Retirement is the beginning of death," he announced. His solution was to join with two former Mars executives, one of them Dean Musser, to start a luxury filled-candy line in 1978. He hoped would it would compare favorably to See's Candies, the renowned California company that was started in 1921 in Los Angeles by a 71-year-old woman.

Forrest put $6 million of his own money into the venture. He was particularly interested in making boxed candy with liquor-flavored centers, ingredients common to European gourmet candies. Since liquor-flavored candies are prohibited in many states, Forrest located his company in Henderson, Nevada, where state law allows the manufacture of candies flavored with such spirits as rum, bourbon and amaretto.

He named the company Ethel M after his mother, who had died at age 97 shortly before the plant opened. Like his father Frank before him, Forrest Sr. made the area above the factory his living quarters, although few Ethel M associates were aware that their legendary boss lived above the store, at 2 Cactus Garden Drive. In fact, between Forrest's reclusiveness and his location in Nevada, people inevitably began calling him the Howard Hughes of the candy industry. One Brach candy company vice president said he had worked in the industry his entire life, had never actually seen Forrest Mars Sr., and only knew a few people—all Mars associates—who had.

Forrest instituted the same policies at Ethel M that he had promulgated at Mars, Inc. There were no reserved parking spaces in the lot and everyone punched a time clock. White uniforms emblemized the cleanliness of the plant.

Although he already insisted on freshness and quality in his candy ingredients, Forrest had to go the extra mile to compete in the luxury candy market. For Ethel M, there could be no mass production or distribution. Gourmet chocolate requires individual attention, fresh ingredients and no preservatives. Its shelf life is a short six weeks: two weeks in the factory, two in the store and two in the customer's home.

Forrest brazenly imitated See's Candies, which dominated the boxed candy business on the West coast. (In the East, Fannie May, Fannie Farmer and Russell Stover share the market.) See's had 150 stores and sold for several dollars less per box than did Ethel M.

Forrest placed Ethel M retail stores in high-traffic locations in nearby states besides Nevada that permitted the sale of liquor-flavored candies: Arizona and California. The liquor candies accounted for about one-quarter of Ethel M's product line and about one-third of its sales.

## Candy Is Dandy, But Liquor Is Quicker

Forrest's first concern was not that Ethel M liquor-flavored candies could not be sold nationwide. He had started the company nearly as a hobby: he wanted the challenge of producing a sophisticated, quality, filled chocolate. Soon, though, the company was engaged in heavy lobbying.

Within a few years, disputes broke out in a number of state legislatures and within the federal Food and Drug Administration over liquor-filled candy. A law dating to 1906 prohibited alcohol in confections. No candy could contain more than .5 percent alcohol by volume, and that alcohol could be derived from extracts only. The law's turn-of-the-century advocates feared that children could get drunk from this type of candy.

An individual state could allow a higher alcohol content, but the candy could only be sold in that state. Confusing the issue were interstate laws which allowed liquor chocolates from Europe to be sold in all states, which seemed unfair to American confectioners.

But since the FDA was no longer enforcing alcohol content laws within states, a number of confectioners were not worried about sales within their states. By the time Ethel M was in business, 15 states and the District of Columbia allowed these candies.

New York had banned alcohol-flavored chocolate during Prohibition. But lobbyists for New York City wanted to entice New Jersey candymakers into the city. They wouldn't relocate because their home state allowed them to manufacture the popular liquor candies that were prohibited in New York.

The controversy focused on two of the three categories of liquor chocolate. One kind uses chocolate shell molds that often resemble miniature bottles and are filled with sugar syrup and liquor. Since this type of confection most closely resembles drinking a liqueur, critics singled it out. In New York, for example, the state considered allowing adults only to buy liquor-filled chocolates—but only if the retail shops had obtained a special license!

Another type of liquor candy is the cordial, which is made by soaking such fruits as cherries or strawberries in liquor, dipping them in a sugar fondant and lastly dipping them in chocolate. The third type has alcohol added into a filling mixture which then is covered with chocolate.

There was less fuss about the cream fillings spiked with liquor than about the other two varieties, and a number of state legislators considered overturning laws prohibiting manufacturers of cream liquor candies from purveying their wares. Ethel M, of course, backed these reform bills.

On the opposing side was NO-ALCC, which stands for the National Organization Against Liquor in Candy for Children. To NO-ALCC, no amount of chocolate can disguise what is an alcoholic drink.

NO-ALCC opposes the introduction of alcohol as an ingredient in chocolate. The admittance of liquor in a confectionery industry product would be a disgrace to the company that promoted the wholesome image of a chocolate bar. "If you're trying to promote candy as a healthy snack, and you put alcohol in it," said one industry official, "it's no longer healthy."

Another manufacturer said that liquor in candy camouflages "an addictive, mind-altering drug." Other candy companies found another argument against liquor candies, pointing out that confections are considered a food item, whereas liquor is a luxury item with different tax scales. Introducing alcohol to candy would make it more difficult to argue the separation and might lead to taxes on all candy.

Both sides admit that a child would more likely be sick before he became drunk on liquor candy. To have the alcoholic equivalent of a can of beer, a child would have to eat nearly 20 filled candies. To get the same amount of liquor as is in one shot of alcohol, a child would have to eat six pounds of candy.

Candy store owners pointed out that this candy is the most expensive on the market. One noted, "At $30 a pound, your average youngster isn't about to come into this store to get a high."

## Apogee

At the beginning of the 70s, a few years before Forrest had decided to retire, five of the country's ten top candy bars were Mars brands: Snickers, Milky Way, 3 Musketeers, M&M's Plain and M&M's Peanut. Although these brands were still popular as the company approached the beginning of the 80s, the future was not so bright. Competition had heightened, large global candy companies were gobbling up smaller companies and competitors were successfully introducing new products. In contrast, Mars was neither buying other candy businesses to keep place with its rivals nor was it, evidently, able to bring out new candies that were as popular as the traditional Mars favorites.

Two new candies that did hit the mark were Starburst Fruit Chews, which were individually wrapped fruit-flavored chews, and Twix Cookie Bars, which consist of caramel over a crunchy cookie, enrobed in milk chocolate. Starburst and Twix remain popular and seem to have found permanent fans. However, many of the new candy products and brand line extensions introduced in the years following Forrest's retirement bombed.

Summit, a cookie bar made of chopped peanuts on top of cream-filled crisp wafers covered with chocolate, was introduced in 1977. It was a one of the first "light" candy bars—and it was a fiasco. Sprint, Mars Double Crunch and Snicker's Peanut Butter Crunch were all failures. An attempt to revive the Forever Yours bar did not fly, either.

In addition, Mars now faced serious competition from Hershey. The Swiss-based Nestlé company also competed seriously against Mars. Rising costs forced confectioners to increase prices and, by the end of the 70s, candy bars cost a quarter, which cut into sales volume.

This contributed to a serious decline in per capita candy consumption during the decade. The amount of candy eaten fell by 25 percent, from about 20 pounds per person in 1968 to 15 pounds by 1980. The reason was not that Americans were substituting fresh fruit for candy. Rather, the pool of heavy candy eaters—children five years to 13 years—declined from nearly 18 percent of the population at the beginning of this period to less than 14 percent by the end.

How could a drop of 5.5 million consumers not hurt candy sales? Even heavy advertising could not compensate for a target audience that had shrunk.

Of course, in Nevada, Forrest Sr. had already anticipated this demographic change by opening Ethel M, the candy line that appealed to adult tastes. In recognition of a lifetime of accomplishment, *Fortune* magazine named him to its Business Hall of Fame.

# Four

# The Successors: Forrest E. Jr. and John F. Mars

An incident in 1980 showed how Mars, Inc. could use its clout to affect what consumers paid for candy—not just for Mars candy but for any of the country's most popular candies. To gain customers and compensate for low per capita candy consumption, Mars moved to increase the size of its candy bars by a hefty ten percent, on average, without increasing the price of the bars. A drop in the cost of cocoa also allowed Mars to lower retail candy prices.

For decades, candy companies had closely mirrored each other's bar weights and prices. Many companies would reduce the size of a bar shortly before raising its cost. When they increased the price, they would restore some or all of the previous weight. The consumer would assume the higher cost was due to the heavier bar.

So not only was the Mars move to raise weight unilaterally unprecedented within the industry, it also threatened a long-standing public image dodge. Mars touted its larger size bars with heavy advertising. The company placed full-page advertisements in every major newspaper across the country and significantly increased its network television ads and spot television ads. The company also benefited from favorable editorials and newspaper columns heralding Mars' bigger bar at no extra cost.

Hershey and other manufacturers took a licking as sales of Mars candy bars—especially their top five, Snickers, Milky Way, 3 Musketeers, M&M's Plain and M&M's Peanut—skyrocketed. Sales of these candy bars rose from between 30 percent to 257 percent when their size increased.

Mars' market share jumped from 37 percent to a stupendous 46 percent in one year. Hershey dropped two percent in market share but was not as badly hurt as such smaller companies as Curtiss and Peter Paul Cadbury. "The Mars move hurt just about everybody," said the president of Cadbury. Still, the other companies did not imitate Mars' actions and increase their bar size.

Mars had achieved its goal. "Consumers came over," said a Mars associate. "We knew that if we improved our value for money, people would buy more of our products. For the consumer, portion size is an important criterion."

Mars scoffed at rumors that it planned to raise candy prices shortly, saying that it would maintain current prices "as long as we can."

A few months later, Mars in fact quietly raised prices from a quarter to thirty cents. Of course, no fanfare or advertising blitz accompanied this turnabout and so most consumers were unaware of the change and continued buying the Mars bars. Also, Mars still had the largest candy bars, even if they were higher in price. So now Mars enjoyed an extra $200 million in revenue, taking 3.4 cents per bar of the five cent rise. And it retained market share.

A furor ignited in the industry over Mars' two-step. Hershey Foods, saying the price increase was unnecessary, took out advertisements charging Mars with an unjustified price hike. Hershey promised to hold its own prices stable.

*Forbes* magazine termed the Mars price rise "brazen" and the action of a "greedy monopolist."

Kmart, which at the time had more than 2,000 stores, and Lucky Stores, with 600, initially refused to stock individual bars of Mars candy. "We understand what Kmart did, but the real boss is the ultimate purchaser and eater of the product," said a Mars associate. "That's who we have to satisfy."

Yet many retailers charge a uniform price for all candy bars, so when Mars raised prices, retailers increased the price of all candy bars they sold. Of course, the extra pennies charged by Mars went back to the company, whereas the surplus that the retailer charged for, say, a Hershey's Milk Chocolate bar went into the retailer's pocket. So Mars' competitors did not profit in any way from the retailers' across-the-board price hikes. In effect, Mars' action imposed a price increase industry-wide that cost consumers a nickel per candy bar and benefited only itself.

Eventually, all the other companies followed suit and raised prices by a nickel, although Hershey was the last to do so.

Such is the power of the mammoth, privately owned Mars company.

## Nestlé's Crunch

There was an even larger, more powerful company on the world stage, however: Nestlé S. A.

Mars and Hershey shared the candy firmament with Nestlé, but the Swiss-based company had found itself caught in a trap in the late 70s that threatened to force it to gnaw off its own foot. Ironically, the snare had been baited and set in the earliest days of the global conglomerate.

American Consul Charles Page founded the Anglo-Swiss Condensed Milk Company in Cham, Switzerland in 1866. Page envisioned his company as taking advantage of Swiss dairy supplies to manufacture the newly invented canned, sweetened milk product. A year later in Vevey, Henri Nestlé began producing cow's-milk infant formula.

In 1877 Page decided to branch into cheese and baby formula; Nestlé, which had sold out to a retired politician, refused Page's buy offer. So Anglo-Swiss opened an American plant and began to loosen its hold on Europe. Nestlé, meanwhile, was adamant about producing only in Switzerland, though it had markets around the globe. At the turn of the century it finally opened plants abroad, first in Norway and then in America, Britain, Germany and Spain. Still, it drew on its Swiss roots sufficiently to tap into that country's famous chocolate industry. In 1905, Anglo-Swiss and Nestlé merged, and the firm that was to become the largest food company on the planet was well on its way.

Through wars and depressions—with their concomitant shortage of milk supplies—fluctuations in the prices of raw materials and the political vagaries of nations, Nestlé always prospered in the long run. At the time when a young Forrest Sr. worked briefly in the Vevey plant, Nestlé was struggling with the new world order; it eventually closed that plant and the original Anglo-Swiss factory in Cham. But the larger effect of the temporary setback was to force the company to decentralize its structure with the parent firm a holding company overseeing the activities of more than 20 subsidiaries on five continents.

In 1938 Nestlé made a breakthrough that would revolutionize the habits of the world: it developed powdered instant coffee, to which it soon added dried tea powder. But the upheavals of World War II threatened its hard-won gains, even while the American armed forces market raised demand for powdered milk. Nestlé shifted part of its management to the U.S.

By the mid 70s, the conglomerate had added a number of other food producers, and was manufacturing soups, seasonings, fruit juices, frozen foods both standard and dietetic, and—above all—the world's first freeze-dried coffee, Taster's Choice. It also had forayed into the non-food arena by taking over L'Oreal cosmetics; Alcon pharmaceuticals and Burton, Parsons contact lenses would soon join the fold.

But at this point there was heard thunder on the left, set off by the very product that had launched Henri Nestlé so long ago: infant formula. Activists pointed out that 21 percent of Nestlé's total formula production took place in developing nations. The problem was that, through aggressive advertising and such time-honored but ethically questionable promotions as supplying hospitals with formula and pressuring them to distribute it to new mothers, Nestlé formula was made to seem superior to mother's milk. The new mothers were encouraged to think formula was more modern—better—than breast milk. Once they had used the formula in the hospital, their lactation slowed down and finally stopped, leaving them entirely dependent on the Nestlé product. But it was expensive, and they were tempted to skimp the amount of powder they mixed into the water; often, the water was contaminated, as well.

To protesters, the company sent a supercilious form letter stating that their formula was wholesome and nutritious when used correctly, disingenuously ignoring the scant likelihood that illiterate, overworked, desperately poor women would be able to use it as it was meant to be under optimum conditions. American and European consumer watchdogs were outraged, and declared a boycott of Nestlé products. It was difficult to maintain, with so many diverse goods coming under the ban, but by the early 80s it was estimated that Nestlé had lost as much as $40 million in sales.

Helmut Maucher, who became managing director in 1981, was determined to stem the flood of disapproval by meeting with boycott groups and making concessions to them. The boycott was rescinded in 1984.

Then, in 1987, Nestlé subsidiary Beech-Nut was found to be adulterating apple juice intended for infant consumption. At the same time, it seemed that the company had gone back to its objectionable practices in the Third World, though Nestlé self-righteously claimed to be adhering to the strict letter of World Health Organization regulations. In 1988 the company was put back on the boycott list.

However, some of the steam seems to have gone out of the moral condemnation engine. The Nestlé advertising ploy perhaps most familiar to the largest number of people today is the continuing saga of the Taster's Choice TV commercial lovers (known in England as the Gold Blend couple, after the British name of the product, and there enjoying a slightly more sophisticated story line than the same actors portray in America). As for their infant formula sales, the company has been so successful in introducing the product in China that it has had to build special roads for transporting the formula from farm to factory and thence to consumers.

In the chocolate world, Nestlé compensated for the problem of maintaining the shelf life of chocolate bars in tropical climates not only by providing its own refrigerated display cases but by developing lower-fat versions of Kit Kat and Smarties, which then have a higher melting point.

But now western-style supermarkets are spreading over the planet like a sci-fi invasionary force, and Nestlé will have to look to its profit margins.

Nestlé accounts for a relatively small but significant portion of the chocolate market in the United States—about ten percent. However, Nestlé is number one in the world in production and sale of packaged foods, coffee and infant formula. By the early 80s, it looked as if it might take away the Mars crown and become the world's largest producer of chocolate, just as Mars had thought it would conquer new lands.

## China M&M's

Mars might be in the ascendant, but that did not mean every single star in its firmament was in a favorable alignment.

Forrest Jr. was beginning to catch on to the fact that his new product introductions, and even his line extensions, were not very popular. The most successful Mars candy bars were the standards: he and John were not able to pull another Snickers brand out of their hat.

It is, after all, very difficult to establish a new brand. Nearly 65 percent of all candy bars sold in the United States are of brands that are more than 50 years old. Consumer awareness of a new confection is expensive to obtain, and consumer habit renders it practically impossible for a new bar to break into the top 20 group of best-selling candy bars.

In order to expand, then, the company would have to move into new territories to sell their mature candy bar brands, such as the popular Milky Way bar. Although Mars had been in business for nearly 60 years by 1980, it had done little exporting because its practice was to set up separate companies and manufacturing plants in the foreign countries to which it was selling.

However, Mars became the first candy company to export to China's friendship stores in 1980. Forrest was elated by his fantastic coup and was delighted to think about the vast Chinese market eating its first Mars product—M&M's.

The company hoped eventually to be able to export its bar candy, too. "That first sale is always the hardest to get," said a Mars associate.

Yet M&M's were seen as a true luxury item by the Chinese. The package size that Mars exported was smaller than the one sold on the American market and cost more, selling for 50 cents. Since the average Chinese worker's monthly income is less than $40, the candy's high price was a serious obstacle to sales.

It remained to be seen whether Mars would discover the key to unlocking the vast resources of the untapped Chinese market.

## Mars Undercover

Just as Mars, Inc. was interested in exporting its products to China, it realized that the time would come when it could sell in Soviet bloc countries, also. Industry experts surmised that, after doing business in China, Mars was looking at the possibility of exporting to other Communist nations. Heeding the demographic slump in the number of children and teens in the United States that had already resulted in a drop in sales, Mars could not ignore the prospect of a low per-capita American consumption stretching into the next century.

The China venture's slow start was clear evidence that entering new cultures was not as easy as simply sending over the goods. Some attention must be paid to identifying the quirks of ethnic groups' tastes and consumption habits, as Forrest Sr. had years before in England.

But why do your own research into a foreign marketplace if you can have a government agency do it for you, free of cost? And while you are at it, why not choose a government agency that has the very best up-to-date information?

Trouble is, the Central Intelligence Agency will not conduct new research or analysis in response to a request, even a Freedom of Information Act request. That's not what FOIA is all about.

But if your father is Forrest Mars Sr., friend of CIA director William J. Casey, it's a lot easier to have your unusual request given special treatment.

So in 1981, Mars filed an FOIA requesting documents on the cocoa and chocolate industry in the USSR and other Warsaw Pact countries. Although the request was unusual, it was duly forwarded to the appropriate office. The staff that ultimately received the inquiry was surprised to see a note attached from the head of their agency, Casey, that asked them to do an unusually complete job of responding to Mars. CIA officials who asked were told that a different procedure was being followed because Bill Casey and Forrest Mars were friends.

The CIA went beyond its typical response. It conducted more than a routine search for Mars and even analyzed information, in what seemed to be violation of federal policy. It supplied Mars with the names, addresses and phone numbers of candy makers in Eastern Bloc countries and gave the company intelligence reports about the Soviet Union's cocoa purchases.

But the data the CIA pulled for the company did not supply figures that Mars had wanted on the amount of imports and exports for cocoa beans, cocoa butter and chocolate liquor by the USSR and eastern bloc countries. So after analyzing material for the company, the agency devised a chart to answer this question.

Of course, the CIA is not supposed to conduct new research in response to FOIA requests, nor does it typically supply any analysis of information that it may have. A 1982 memorandum to all employees notes the federal standard of ethics that states, "Government employees should avoid taking any action which may result in or create the appearance of . . . giving preferential treatment."

Although the CIA had taken only a few short weeks to put relevant material together and evaluate information for Mars, the data ended up not being helpful to the company. After having rushed their analysis, the CIA took three years to clear the material for forwarding to Mars. By the time the company received the requested information, it was irrelevant.

## *E.T. : The Extraterrestrial*

In 1982, Mars suffered an embarrassment that associates talk about to this day. Under Forrest Jr. and John, the company had become so rigid that managers were both fearful of taking risks and had become out-of-touch regarding new creative marketing techniques. So when the producers of an upcoming movie contacted the image-wary McLean headquarters in 1982 to see if it would like M&M's to be featured as the candy that cements a friendship between an extraterrestrial creature and a young boy, Mars said no. The executive who made the decision felt that he could get in trouble for green-lighting a product placement that might not justify the expense for the unproven movie *E.T.*

For its products to be seen by millions of moviegoers, a company can either pay a placement fee or be a marketing/production partner with the studio. It is a complicated procedure with no rate card to simplify how much a product placement will cost the sponsoring company. In the 80s, the expense for a direct placement ad usually ranged from 50 cents to one dollar per thousand moviegoers, with a typical range of $25,000 to $100,000 in fees. Part of the cost is determined by how prominently the product is shown. Obviously, in the case of *E.T.*, the fee would be high because of the importance of the candy in the screenplay's storyline.

When Mars said no to the placement, Steven Spielberg's company wrote out M&M's. Instead, they substituted Hershey's Reese's Pieces, a peanut butter candy that is also encased in a hard candy shell. Hershey liked *E.T.* and put promotional dollars behind it. Sales of Reese's Pieces jumped 70 percent the month after the film's release. In addition, kids wanted to be able to snack on the same candy as *E.T.* while watching the movie: 800 movie theaters that had never carried Reese's Pieces began to stock the candy as a regular theater-counter offering.

Just as important was the missed opportunity for M&M's to gain exposure, through both the movie and subsequent video rentals, and to be linked to the most lovable sales creature in memory.

Mars eventually spoke to their error, justifying it by saying the company did not have time to work on the project "at the time the film was being negotiated" because they were planning for sponsorship of the 1984 Olympics. Company officials patted their own backs—simultaneously attempting to cover their backsides—by saying, "We felt that we were doing much more through our Olympic sponsorship to help develop future generations of young athletes."

## *ET* 2— The Entertainment Tonight Gambit

Besides sponsoring Olympic and other athletic events, Mars uses promotional gimmicks to hook young consumers. One such contrivance backfired in the early 80s. Candy customers were told that they could exchange ten Starburst

Fruit Chews wrappers for a poster of either Shaun Cassidy, Linda Ronstadt or Cheryl Ladd. Unfortunately, the company had never received permission from the celebrities for this promotion.

Both Cassidy and Ronstadt sued, charging that their names and likenesses were used to imply that they endorsed Starburst Fruit Chews, and that this use was unauthorized. Although the company, in legal papers, claimed that "Mars' advertising philosophy for many years has been to avoid using any spokesperson for its products and . . . does not currently advertise any endorsement of any of its products by any famous personality," it was clear that its rationale did not wash.

Regardless of the company's protestation of innocence, Mars decided to settle out of court rather than fight the lawsuits. Cassidy settled for $10,000 and Ronstadt was paid $32,000.

## The Average Joe . . . or John, or Forrest

Few associates at Mars, Inc. have ever laid eyes on Forrest Sr. The top Mars managers who had been required to report to him were, naturally, always a little nervous around the boss, especially since they feared he might, without warning, lead them in prayer or belittle them in front of others. But despite Forrest's negative traits, the Mars associates respected the vigorous athletic man who had built a tremendous international candy company as well as a worldwide pet food firm, a rice business and even an electronic vending machine enterprise.

Forrest Jr. and John lacked many of their father's positive attributes. Least important cosmically, but vital in an image-conscious world, is the fact that neither man is impressive-looking. Although this is partly a matter of genetics, the men's paunches, slumped posture and polyester-blend suits do little to improve on what nature did not give them.

They also shared a characteristic that their employees felt was odd. Despite their having grown up at Marland, an impressive estate of 600 acres, each man insisted on speaking of himself as the average working Joe, just another salaried employee. Once John remarked sharply, "If you've figured out a way to make a living without working, I'd certainly like to know."

Since everyone knew that John and Forrie had each been given a one-third share of a half-billion dollar business—by then worth much more—the brothers' statements met with a silent response of "Who are they trying to kid?" The brothers' attempts at being humble did not go over well with fellow workers or neighbors. Yet many who know the Marses believe that the men actually perceive themselves as middle class.

On the plus side, neither man demanded perquisites that many executives expected in the greedy days of the 80s. Of course, part of their restraint may have been due to being owners of a family business; few family business heirs use their own companies' funds on, for instance, corporate jet planes to whisk them to meetings. They know that these costs ultimately come from their own pockets.

But the brothers' lack of pretension was, and is, so extreme that it seems inappropriate. For instance, neither brother likes to use a car and driver, preferring to take the wheel themselves. And when they rent a car, it's an inexpensive sedan. Neither they nor their associates ever fly first class.

This mean and stingy approach to travel is especially peculiar in the case of John, who—with the rice, pet food and money machine businesses to manage—is constantly on the road. In fact, his lunch dates are booked one full year in advance. Division heads who fall behind in their lines' return rate can expect a monthly visit from one of the brothers until he does better. But John has been known to visit company sites traveling by Winnebago, for example, so that he could sleep in the vehicle in the plant's parking lot and avoid the cost of a motel room.

Lunch for the brothers at the McLean office is a solitary sandwich at a neighborhood luncheonette, coffee shop or the nearby Hardee's. If a visiting associate is in town, one of the brothers might drive him to a restaurant to talk business over lunch—separate checks, of course.

Their clothes, too, are sometimes an embarrassment. Neither man seems to have heard of custom tailoring, or even of such quality ready-to-wear stores as Brooks Brothers or Nordstrom—both within 15 miles of their office—where men who are not worth billions or even millions shop.

Instead, the brothers prefer synthetic-blend, off-the-rack suits that go with their thick-soled Corfam shoes, worn until they sport holes. John's eyeglass frames are always several years behind the fashion, and the red blazer that he favored in the 80s made him look like a car salesman on Labor Day. Associates in other cities will wear threadbare clothes to work when they know one of the Mars brothers is in town, fearing they may be criticized for being too sartorially splendid.

Nor is their modest business style a cover-up for an indulgent personal lifestyle. For many years the family policy was to put profits back into the company. In the early 80s, the three Mars siblings received only nominal dividends. The brothers' salaries were only about $650,000 at this time, which is small in proportion to the size of their company.

Forrest Jr. drove a Plymouth station wagon that racked up nearly 100,000 miles before his mother Audrey gave him a blue Mercedes. In 1983, after their four daughters had left home, he and Virginia did move out of the house they'd lived in for 15 years. They bought a slightly showier 10-room townhouse in McLean's Merrywood development. The area was prestigious, as Merrywood had been the Auchincloss estate where Jacqueline Bouvier grew up and where John F. Kennedy, then a United States senator, had written *Profiles in Courage* with Arthur Schlesinger's help while recuperating from surgery. But even in Merrywood the Forrest Marses were still close to the "shop."

John and Adrienne, too, lived within ten minutes of the headquarters office, at 4137 North River Street in McLean, in an upper-middle class neighborhood called Chain Bridge Forest. John would also drive himself to work—in a Jeep.

## Managerial Shock Waves

Loyalty to Mars, Inc. from its associates was wearing thin.

For one thing, it was nearly impossible for an associate to establish a relationship with the brothers—even if the associate had wanted to. One professional man in the Washington area said, "I've known Forrest Jr. on and off for years, but I really don't think I can say I know him very well."

Since each brother played favorites, each would have a retinue surrounding him. Its members knew not to disagree with either man, as their manner and essence were both dictatorial. And if an associate made Forrest or John angry, their immediate bosses would leave them twisting in the wind, too fearful of the brothers to defend their subordinate.

Under Forrest Sr., the company had at least enjoyed a reputation for never letting anyone go without cause. A man could work for the firm for his entire career. Now, under Forrest Jr. and John, jobs seemed less secure.

Shock waves reverberated throughout the business when a 20-year veteran, Alun Jones, was fired. Jones had worked his way up to the company's presidency, where he remained for only one year before his dismissal. Gossip never pinpointed the exact reason for Jones' downfall: it could have been due to the brothers' skittishness at Hershey's breathing down their necks for market share. Or was Jones too interested in innovations for the brothers' sense of security? Perhaps it was because Jones violated the company's fanaticism for secrecy by talking to the press; that alone is justification for dismissal at Mars, Inc.

If one reason for Jones's firing could be identified, it would probably be the turnaround that Hershey had played on Mars in late 1983, when it raised its candy bar prices from 30 to 35 cents. Just as when Mars had increased their prices from 25 to 30 cents in 1980, and retailers decided to raise prices on all candy bars, when Hershey raised prices to 35 cents in 1983 the retailers again increased the cost of all candy bars to 35 cents. Hershey got the extra pennies for its bars and the retailers pocketed the nickel profit it made on the rest of the candy bars.

Everyone waited for Jones to raise prices so that the retailers would have to turn the extra money over to Mars. But he refused to, figuring that there were enough retail outlets that had not yet raised the prices of non-Hershey candy. Consumers, he felt, would notice and favor Mars candy over Hershey candy.

This never happened: Mars candy sales did not increase and the company was losing nearly $5 million a month due to the 30-cent line that Jones maintained. Soon after Jones left, Mars candy bars were marked up to 35 cents.

In addition to Jones's dismissal, the sales and marketing director were reassigned in a dual step that amounted to demotions.

No matter what the reason for letting Jones go and reassigning other executives, these actions signaled to managers a new and less secure era for Mars associates. In the past, they had put up with a number of eccentricities on the part of the Mars men because of their high pay and their job protection. Now, they were as vulnerable to being fired as anyone else in the industry.

## "Rat Poison in Mars Bars"— *The Sunday Times*, London

Only a generation ago, trick-or-treaters could be given unwrapped candy and even homemade goodies. Now, hospitals routinely offer x-ray services on Halloween to check for razor-spiked apples, and careful parents discard any sweets that are not in intact hygienic coverings. Though this development strikes a particular chill to the heart, with its unsavory invasion of anonymous modern mayhem into the would-be innocent revels of children, in fact there have been no incidents of deliberate mass contamination of candy in America. Elsewhere, however, that barrier has been breached.

No matter how little sympathy associates had for Forrest Jr. and John after the headquarters upheaval, everyone was shocked and scared by the news they heard from England in late 1984. The Animal Liberation Front had delivered letters to the British Broadcasting Company, to the *Sunday Times* and to the *Mirror* threatening the safety of Mars candy products.

The letters said that their packets enclosed poisoned Mars candy bars and they warned that other Mars bars injected with rat poison had been placed on store shelves in London, York, Leeds, Coventry and Southampton. A few of the bars were marked, so as to be easily recognized and removed from the shelves before a consumer could purchase them. The marked bars carried a cross on the bottom of the wrapper and a six-paragraph leaflet inside, but other Mars candy bars had no feature to identify them as having been impregnated with poison.

The leaflets read, in part, "Read carefully: This is not a joke. This confectionery has been adulterated."

The animal rights extremists claimed that their actions were protests against experiments that the Mars U.K. Ltd. was conducting on monkeys. In response, Mars declared that they did not use animals in experiments. Scotland Yard was immediately called by the media who had received the threatening letters and the adulterated candy bars. Detectives at the Yard said they were treating the threat seriously and were in the process of analyzing the candy.

Acting quickly, the company removed its candy bars from the shelves of retail stores in Manchester, Leeds, Salisbury, Blandford (Dorset), Dorchester and Lytchett Minster (Dorset). Typically, about three million Mars bars are eaten each day in England, so such swift, concerted action was required to protect the public.

In addition, Mars, Inc. considered removing as many as 10 million candy bars from display in order to examine them for signs of puncturing or for breaks in their heat-sealed wrappers.

A 14-year old girl and a young boy had already consumed tampered-with Mars candy bars before they saw the warning leaflet enclosed by the Animal Liberation Front. Fortunately, they suffered no reaction or ill-effect other than a severe scare.

This was not the first time the English had been intimidated by this extremist group. In July, the Animal Liberation Front had contaminated shampoo made by a company that allegedly used animals for testing by pouring bleach into the detergent. The group had also claimed responsibility for syringes filled with rat poison placed in London supermarkets. They freed minks from mink farms and, more seriously, they broke into laboratories, assaulting lab workers with crowbars and sledgehammers. In that incident, three people were hospitalized. They also threatened to break into scientists' homes, smash their hands to pulp, and shoot them in front of their families. When the group telephoned the media during the Mars bar poisonings, they used the same identifying codeword employed during the earlier threats.

On the second day of the scare, Mars disclosed that it actually had funded a project at Guy's Hospital in London involving monkeys. The monkeys were given a sugar-rich diet as part of research into tooth decay. In exchange for conducting these studies, the hospital received £25,000 from the company.

Mars denied that the monkeys were force-fed candy or maltreated in any way, and insisted that the experiments had been conducted under the supervision of the Home Office. "The highest standards of humane treatment" were followed, a Mars spokesperson said. In fact, the testing had been completed three months earlier and no further work with animals was planned.

There was one small comfort derived from investigation of the incident. The police were confident that the candy bars emerging from the factory at Slough were intact and had not been doctored until after they reached retail shops. At least Mars workers were not implicated in the threat.

Although testing was inconclusive, Scotland Yard announced that people should not be alarmed, since no one had yet been poisoned. The Yard did caution consumers to use caution in purchasing Mars candy "until we or Mars can give further advice." One Member of Parliament praised the reaction of Mars officials, calling Mars "an exceptionally responsible and worthy company" for having dispatched 1,000 members of its sales and merchandising force to help shopkeepers and wholesalers check their stock. No Mars bars manufactured in England were exported to the United States.

Of course, the animal rights extremists gained no friends or sympathizers through their threatening actions. Even those who were opposed to animal experiments were outraged at the attack on innocent human beings and, especially, children. Particularly frightening was this escalation of violence against the public over a short period of time, ironic in a country with perhaps the strongest animal protection laws in the world. The Under-Secretary of State at the Home Office issued a statement: "It beggars belief that these people are prepared to sacrifice children on the altar of their own fanaticism. They need to be caught. Someone must know who they are, and I urge members of the public to help the police if they can."

To cap official reaction to the threat, the Royal Society for the Prevention of Cruelty to Animals roundly condemned the Animal Liberation Front outright, calling the actions totally irresponsible and corrupt.

## Rat Tart

Scotland Yard had tested the Mars candy bars enclosed in the threatening letters from the Animal Liberation Front to the media and found traces of rat poison in two of them. However, none of the Mars bars that were removed from retail shelves were contaminated. Since the two children who had eaten the marked candy bars were also free of poisoning symptoms, the government declared that the action was a hoax.

Although everyone breathed a sigh of relief—especially at Mars, Inc.—the incident could not be swept out of mind. Animal rights militants were escalating a violent campaign with the help of young English anarchists. Disenchanted youth from slum areas were supposedly using the animal rights cause as an excuse for anarchist-inspired attacks on big business. It was planned as economic sabotage.

"They are out to smash the system as much as they are out to rescue animals," said the Royal Society for the Prevention of Cruelty to Animals.

The Front claims to have 1,500 activists and 1,200 supporters without having a formal administration or membership. Instead, the organization uses a structure polished by Bolshevik revolutionaries in Russia: they operate in a series of small groups or cells, and newcomers are restricted to low-key activities until they become trusted members of the cell.

This organizing principle both insulates the larger group and its higher echelons from massive betrayal by infiltrators, and makes recruitment on the lowest levels easy and relatively risk-free. So the menace was growing, and even the most radical of establishment animal-rights groups, the British Union for the Abolition of Vivisection, withdrew its support of the Animal Liberation Front and condemned the Mars Bar hoax as "irresponsible."

Mars, Inc. informed the financial community that after a significant early drop in candy bar sales, their figures had rebounded. And the president of an English company called Product Safety, which advises manufacturers on how to fight back against this type of menace, reported that his phone had not stopped ringing.

Much like other companies in the United Kingdom, Mars had been subject to a more mundane sort of threat. Four years earlier, a man had been prosecuted for threatening to bomb the company's factory in Slough unless it paid £30,000 in ransom. The Mars associate who received the call asked whether the extortionist meant 30,000 one-pound notes.

"What do you think I mean," said the man indignantly, "30,000 Mars bars?"

Although no similar dangers to public safety developed that specifically involved Mars products, the company continued to be the target of terrorist menaces by animal rights extremists. Shopkeepers who sold Mars candy were threatened with smashed windows and glued door locks. Eventually, however, these attempts at intimidation died away.

## Staying Lean at McLean

Although the poisoning hoax had all the Mars U.K. associates in turmoil, it attracted little press attention in the United States. Business went on as usual in McLean, save for the brothers' immediate attention and that of a few top managers.

After the crisis wound down, the days resumed their former routine. And although Forrest Sr. was no longer calling his sons with criticism and advice, the company still bore his unmistakable stamp.

Employees, as one example, are still called associates. Nevertheless, as one man remarked, "They call them associates but they treat them like dogs."

Both of Forrest's sons, by now men in their 50s, punched in each morning just as every Mars associate must do to this day. John, the workaholic, is often at the unmarked McLean building by 6:30 a.m. (In the mid-80s, headquarters moved from 1651 Old Meadow Road in McLean to its current site on Elm Street.) Both John and Forrest Jr. work on the second floor, in a large room that more closely resembles the open atmosphere of a daily paper's newsroom than the executive floor of a multinational company.

High-ranking Mars associates are also still expected to keep to a grueling schedule. One former marketing manager said, "The view was at Mars you would pay one person two salaries to do the work of three. It was a very lean place."

It is easy for Forrest and John to keep an eye on the hours of their associates, between the punch card system and the fact that, at headquarters, neither man has a private office. Instead, they sit at functional black metal desks at the back of this huge open room. Not even partitions separate the fifty-odd headquarters associates, who must keep their voices down when talking on the telephone to avoid complete babble and to maintain some semblance of confidentiality. Although desk chairs are upholstered, any extra chairs are molded plastic reminiscent of the kind found in elementary schools. There are four conference rooms on the floor but they are glass-walled. The conference rooms are usually not busy as meetings are to take place on a strict as-needed basis. There is no privacy on this floor.

At each manufacturing site, division heads are seated in a circular pattern so that they can communicate directly with each other. Their physical placement is symbolic of the message that they should work together and not resort to interpreting their tasks too narrowly.

Forrest Jr. and John share a secretary. No one is assigned a secretary to himself or herself. In fact, Mars associates pick up their own phones and make their own photocopies. Few desks have computers, for writing memos is against corporate policy. Forrest Jr. and John feel that memos are a waste of time and that thoughts are better communicated in person or over the phone. In addition, their penchant for security makes them wary of seeing Mars business committed to writing.

Of course, both men travel a great deal. Richard Berezden, a physics professor at American University who knew Forrest when Berezden was president of the university, said, "What I discovered is that the man seems to live on airplanes.

He's eternally in motion." Several times a year, the brothers forgo their travels and have their world-flung associates come to them.

"McLean Week" is a dreaded occasion for most associates. That's when all the top associates fly in for meetings and strategic planning. This is not a warm and cozy occasion where bonding takes place. During McLean Week, or while the brothers travel extensively, they are present at dozens of oral presentations. But their associates are unnerved by the brothers' seeming inattention to what they are being told. "You would work desperately hard getting your presentation ready for them," a British former executive remembers. "But while you are trying to get your point over, they carry on talking or just look out of the window as though they are not interested."

On the other hand, if the associate dares to stop talking, Forrest Jr. or John have been known to start yelling obscenities and ordering the unnerved associate to keep talking until one of the brothers tells him to stop.

At these meetings, current-day managers know not to spend extensive time preparing vivid graphics. John, who feels presentation charts are a waste of time, flew into a rage that would have done justice to his father when he found out that an associate had spent two or three hours working on graphics for a meeting. In front of other staff, John ripped up the charts and berated the hapless executive.

In general, the human element seems to be considered a necessary evil at best by the brothers. Although some associates give John credit for stressing state-of-the-art automation in its plants, others have joked that his primary aim was not efficiency but rather a person-less workforce.

Even Mars associates who never come into contact with the brothers have feared their wrath. One metropolitan Washington, D.C. sales representative, whose part-time position working for the company entailed checking on Mars candy placement in drugstores and grocery stores, had to resort to personal pleading in convincing McLean retailers to stock a new Munch Peanut bar (since dropped by the company). Yes, she admitted, it was an unpopular new brand. But it was one that John Mars favored and woe would betide her if he stopped into a local store and did not see it on the shelf.

## The Sayings of the Co-Presidents Mars

Forrest Jr. and John proudly claim that they are vigilant in supporting the traditional Mars values. To this end, they have actually encapsulated the key attributes that make Mars different from other companies—institutionalizing their father's work ethic and crystallizing their beliefs—into five principles.

The standard supported by the brothers in practice as well as theory is that of **quality**, which is the first commandment of Mars. No exceptions to the policy of choosing the best ingredient can ever be allowed, for Forrest Jr. and John feel that any deviation could lead to another deviation and soon the company would have lowered its overall standards. **Quality** also keeps Mars manufacturing candy bars under conditions of pristine cleanliness. If someone even suspects that a huge candy batch has been contaminated by a foreign object having been ground up with the other ingredients, the candy is tossed, even if the possible contamination would not cause health problems to a consumer. Even the floors of the company's pet food factories are constantly measured for bacteria, using higher standards than hospitals.

**Responsibility** is the second principle. It translates to hard work and the freedom to make decisions. Forrest Jr. reflected this when he said in a public speech, "My brother and I believe we work for our associates, and not the other way around."

Less charming is the chopping block prominently placed on the headquarters' second floor. Its brass plate reads: "Head on the block responsibility."

(Yet increasingly managers were feeling that they had responsibility but not the authority that should go with it. Forrest Sr. had decentralized the Mars company years before flatter organizational structures became popular. Yet now, Forrest Jr. and John were concentrating authority at the top. Also, while successful businesses encourage their managers and employees not to be afraid of taking chances, the Mars chopping block certainly gives a different message.)

**Mutuality** is a value expressing cooperation and the philosophy that everyone wins in a successful business encounter. On the other hand, the brothers' emphasis on their products being number one in whatever market they entered was unrealistic. In practice, each of the brothers wanted to be top dog.

**Efficiency** is a principle that has led to the company's high profit margin. Yet it looks as though efficiency is now working against the business. The mature Mars candy bar brands, such as Snickers bars, are produced at such high manufacturing and marketing levels that a new brand could take years before equaling the volume of a Snickers. By being a company that is production-driven, and by stressing return on total assets, Mars has limited itself to manufacturing its mature brands on a massive scale.

The fifth principle is behind the siblings' consensus never to sell shares in Mars, Inc. The reason is **Freedom,** which can best be achieved through private and closely held ownership. The family refuses to mortgage its future for growth today; they would rather sacrifice the present. While another company's strategic plan may cover any time from the next year to the next five years, Mars' long-range planning covers a quarter-century. Freedom also gives Forrest Jr. and John the ability to ignore Wall Street and the media and allows them nondisclosure of assets, profit and debt.

Forrest Jr. once gave a speech to business majors at Duke University, a school some of the fourth-generation Mars children have attended. He expounded on privacy, using phrasing the company will also write to reporters requesting interviews, saying that privacy is "morally and ethically proper and even desirable, and a key to healthy, normal living."

Privacy and secrecy have deeper implications for a business that likes to see itself as a family unit. Psychologists warn against family secrets because their keeping is usually not healthy or functional for the individual members within the family unit. Similarly, there are drawbacks to working for a company with a restrictive behavior code.

A report released in the early 80s by the International Union of Food and Allied Workers noted that "the Mars employee is encouraged to feel like a member—though not necessarily like an adult member—of a 'big Mars family.' On the other hand, this 'family relationship' is exploited to stimulate efficiency."

Mars, Inc. points to its company's lack of unionization to reinforce their picture of a contented workforce. It has been more than 30 years since a union was able to get so far as to call a representation election. Although this image of a non-unionized Mars is generally true, few people know that the California Kal Kan plant was unionized. Its workers amount to an extremely small percentage of the Mars work force, however. Although the Mars family is not known for hefty contributions to causes, their family foundation has given money regularly to the anti-union National Right to Work Legal Defense Fund.

The missing Mars principle is **Innovation**. The brothers lack their father's fearlessness in risk-taking, a characteristic that drove him to develop new products, acquire brand lines and diversify the company into electronics, pet food and rice. Instead, the brothers give only the appearance of innovation as they develop such novelty bars as the 3 Musketeers Ice Cream Bars that are really mere spinoffs of their decades-old candy bars.

## Dealing with the Reality

The Five Principles are a lot more lofty than Forrest Jr. and John's actual behavior, which starts at unattractive, moves towards creepy and oscillates all the way to peculiar. Their father's withdrawal from the company only served to exacerbate the rivalry between the brothers, which heightened their odd behavior. Because the brothers see each other as competitors, the associates working for the company in either the candy divisions or the other businesses follow suit and group themselves into either the Forrest Jr. or the John camp.

The feeling is that Forrest Jr. is more difficult to work with than John. Although he has a number of positive traits—he has a personal life that he values and he is more sociable with associates—he also has a number of negatives. He has a terrible temper and does not hesitate to let his anger loose on whomever is around.

Forrest Jr. is the more secretive of the two men, to the point of irrationality. One man who had worked with Forrest Jr. caught a glimpse of him at National Airport, on his way to catch a flight.

"Forrest!," the man called out, trying to get his attention. "Forrest Mars!"

Forrest Jr. heard his name being called, glanced over and recognized his friend, and walked over to him. However, Forrest Jr. was not happy.

"How dare you call my name out loud in a crowded airport," he said angrily. "I'm traveling under a false name!"

John has the advantage of being the brighter of the two men. Even his father—the man who values intelligence more than other traits—would express this, indicating he had only one son with brains.

"Forrest is . . . ," Forrest Sr. would pause dramatically, "well, Forrest is a nice boy . . . but no brains. Now John," and Forrest would close his eyes halfway and say with a touch of sarcasm, "John may make something of himself."

John may be bright but he is also stubborn. Perhaps being the shorter of the brothers—he is 5'10" to Forrie's 6"1"—has made him touchy. For whatever reason, he wearies his managers by being more than willing to argue a point endlessly. He is brusque and cold and nearly anti-social, as seen by what one associate said was his "propensity to belch, pick his nose, or take off his socks and shoes during meetings."

But both men are "cold," according to someone who knows them well. "Cold to people outside the family?" he was asked.

"Oh, God, yes," he said. "But they're cold to insiders, too."

## Candy Freeze

Forrest had reason to worry about his sons' potential. By 1985, the candy EKG was flat. Other companies had been looking around to find new but related food areas to move into to compensate for the slow candy market. Also, candy sales are cyclical, peaking at Christmas and Halloween and leaving long lower periods during much of the rest of the year. It made sense for candy manufacturers to consider snacks and ice cream, as consumers tend to blur the distinction between those categories and candy. In fact, a confectionery trade journal had already declared, "Candy isn't an industry in itself anymore."

Snack foods and ice cream novelties looked attractive to such candy companies as Hershey Foods and Nestlé. Nestlé produced a Nestlé Crunch ice cream bar and, by 1986, had added a Quik bar, chocolate ice cream covered in milk chocolate. L.S. Heath & Sons Inc. had been selling ice cream products for a number of years; its Heath ice cream bar was well-liked by consumers.

Mars, however, lagged behind other confectionery companies. It was neither competing in the $450 million granola bar market nor the $1.7 billion ice cream novelty market, both of which had grown in leaps in the early 80s. By 1985, for example, ice cream novelties were a $900 million market growing at the rate of ten percent a year, faster than any other grocery store product. And Mars was not part of this explosion.

Its devotion to its core business had become legendary and it was uncomfortable with a wide product mix. When Mars U.K. Ltd. became interested in potato sticks, rather than develop the product itself, it spun off a new company called Dornay, which was not successful.

## Nuts and Flakes

Mars finally entered the granola snack bar market in 1986. By the time the company introduced its first crunchy granola bar—Kudos Wholegrain Bars—other food manufacturers had been selling this health-inspired snack food for a decade. Most of the companies in the granola bar market were package-goods or cereal companies; for example, General

Mills produced the popular Nature Valley bar. By 1986, Quaker Oat Company, primarily a cereal business, dominated the granola bar market and enjoyed nearly a 50 percent market share with Quaker Chewy granola bars and Granola Dipps.

Granola bars shot skyward in popularity when producers added chocolate and peanut butter, realizing that the dry bars needed juicing up. These ingredients made the bar better tasting and improved its texture. Granola bars, even when covered with chocolate, still outranked candy bars for nutritional value, a fact that appealed to consumers.

Since Mars lagged behind the other manufacturers, it poured money into support of its new brand, the first national product introduction of the company's since Twix Cookie Bars in 1976, ten years earlier. Mars was rumored to be spending about $50 million on the Kudos launch. However large its advertising and promotion budget, industry analysts felt Mars was entering the market too late. For instance, with its New Trail bar introduced in 1982, confectionery Hershey Foods had already auspiciously jumped ahead of Mars. There had been years of growth when the granola bar was a new product but, by 1986, the market was saturated.

More important, Mars announced that Kudos would be the first in a long line of new products aimed at breaking out of the division's traditional candy market. Snack foods, after all, were annually generating $27 billion and Mars was drooling.

## DoveBar and "Aimainaimze"

Later that same year, Mars announced its purchase of DoveBars International Inc., maker of a pricey 500-calorie ice cream bar called the DoveBar that is hand-dipped in rich chocolate. Mars had never had as strong a presence in acquisitions as did other candy companies. Hershey Foods, for example, owned nearly 800 Friendly restaurants that were prized for the Friendly ice cream, already using Reese's Peanut Butter Cups and Pieces in their desserts and take-home pints. Mars' conservative policy of avoiding debt kept it from acquiring other companies.

Tootsie Roll Industries, a public company with 50 percent ownership by the Gordon family, was able to avoid long-term debt during this period while also acquiring other candy companies such as the Mason division of Candy Corporation of America (Mason Dots) and Cella Confectioners (chocolate covered cherries), the Charms Company, Junior Mints, Charleston Chew, and Sugar Daddies and Sugar Babies.

Tootsie Roll Industries is the world's largest maker of lollipops, making 16 million every day, including Blow Pops, Tootsie Pops and Charms. Additionally, it manufactures 40 million Tootsie Rolls each day, 15 million Mason Mints and 20 million Dots.

Like the Marses, the Gordons also run their candy business en famille: Melvin Gordon is chairman and chief executive officer and Ellen Rubin Gordon is president and chief operating officer. In addition to their successful acquisitions, Tootsie Roll also has developed strong line extensions, a concept Mars has found problematic.

Now, finally, Mars was buying a prestigious ice cream novelty business. The DoveBar had started in Chicago in the 30s by Leo Stefanos, proprietor of a candy store, who hand-dipped vanilla ice cream into liquid chocolate. For many years, the self-indulgent could find their rich ice cream treat only in Chicago because Stefanos had no interest in expanding outside the region. When Mars bought the company from his heirs in 1985, it had $20 million in sales.

Both companies were family businesses with product quality as their most important asset. Mike Stefanos, Leo's son, stayed with the ice cream company after its acquisition by Mars and he predicted that his DoveDippers would be hand-dipping 35 million DoveBars and DoveDelights in the upcoming year. On the Mars side, the new venture was a comfortable fit for a secretive company that needed to rejuvenate its product line.

As another strategy, the company decided to use M&M's to compete directly against the Smarties candies, which were sold throughout Europe. Smarties' shell is softer than M&M's' shell and the candy is packaged in a tube, not a bag. (In the early 90s, an unhappy Princess of Wales used the well-known Smarties as a metaphor to describe the demands placed upon her: "I'm the biggest prostitute in the world. I'm handed 'round like a tube of Smarties.")

M&M's had been sold in Europe since 1983, with varying degrees of cultural adaptation required for effective marketing. Its introduction to the French included an information campaign explaining how to pronounce the unfamiliar name: "aimainaimze."

Already, many traditional Mars products had been made a part of the candy culture in the Netherlands, Italy, Austria, Germany, France and Belgium. Although the candy bars tasted familiar to American tourists, the wrappers confused them. Milky Way bars are one of Europe's favorites but their wrapper says they are Mars bars. The 3 Musketeers bar is called Milky Way bar.

M&M's had never been manufactured in the United Kingdom although Mars had produced similar sweets—Treets and Minstrels—that it was planning to discontinue. (This was not a difficult decision: Treets had never done well, ranking 50th among British sweets.)

Mars had been slipping in the English market and now was in the number three position, behind Rowntree Mackintosh with nearly a 27 percent market share, and Cadbury Schweppes, in the lead with 31 percent. Rowntree had just toppled Mars bars from being England's most popular candy with its Kit Kat bar. Mars was planning a comeback with M&M's candies and was making it the country's most expensive candy launch, at $11 million.

Mars had several options: develop a new brand or introduce a brand unknown to the British. Given the company's semi-successful record at developing new brands, it made more sense in the short- term for Mars to bring M&M's to the English.

## Not Just Kid Stuff

Meanwhile, America was graying. Consumer tastes were shifting, moving parallel with the demographic change of the late 80s that reflected the greater numbers of people 40 and older. Mars was finding that adults prefer a different type of candy to that favored by children and teenagers.

Snickers bar still ranked as the country's most popular candy bar but American adults were getting pickier about the quality of the chocolate they ate. European companies saw this as an open invitation: Nestlé, Cadbury Schweppes and Huhtamaki of Finland were all becoming formidable competitors of Mars. Nestlé's Alpine bar, for example, was developed to appeal to a more mature taste and was given its fancy name and packaging.

On the domestic front, Hershey began advertising its Hershey's Golden Almond and Golden III brands in the glossy magazine *The New Yorker*. It also did well with the Hershey's Big Block brand, which was a special hit with adult men.

In addition to the new bars catering to mature tastes, brands were pulled out of storage and repackaged as nostalgia items: Warner Lambert's American Chicle division brought back Beeman's, Black Jack and Clove brand gums.

Mars responded with typical caution. It began testing Royals mints, a mint chocolate shelled in hard candy, rather like M&M's.

## Shooting Stars

As more fissures began showing in the Mars facade, the company that spent heavily on advertising began to question its agencies as it saw its market share slip. In 1985, the company became uncomfortable with D'Arcy MacManus Masius' Worldwide. The agency had been formed in the 70s through a series of mergers and was a natural for Mars' English business because Masius in London had been the first and primary shop for Mars.

However, after the merger some felt that the company did not meld its offices into a unified group. "The lack of cohesion at D'Arcy was particularly anathema to Mars, given the company's personality," said a former D'Arcy official. The iron-fisted management style of Forrest Jr. and John was unable to stand any sense of ambiguity.

Although Mars increased its advertising spending by nearly 14 percent in 1985, it continued to fret over the rise in mergers of advertising agencies, with one of the agencies almost acting as a holding company for the group. It was feared that there would be account conflict problems. The planned Saatchi & Saatchi acquisition of Ted Bates Worldwide brought into question the rival account of Cadbury USA with Saatchi, which handled the Mounds, Almond Joy and York Peppermint Patty brands, with the Mars account that was at Bates and included M&M's, Snickers, Milky Ways, Kal Kan and Uncle Ben's rice brands.

Saatchi ultimately decided not to merge the two shops, and it gave up its Nestlé and Rowntree accounts. The ad agencies, of course, maintained that there were no real clashes in handling accounts for competing companies in the same industry. At the same time, they recognized that the companies themselves may have had a different perspective on the situation. One account executive said, "While we don't accept there is a conflict because we are autonomous, there is no doubt Mars will not live with other chocolate-based confectionery products anywhere in the group."

Mars continued to pressure Saatchi to get rid of its Cadbury account at D'Arcy and, in the end, overhauled its advertising after pulling more than $40 million of billings from two of its biggest United States shops. The Mars candy account was lost by Leo Burnett USA because the agency also handled other companies that manufactured pet food. Mars prefers to have a small number of agencies that can handle both pet food and candy, due to its belief that a small group is more efficient and that its accounts can be controlled more closely.

Backer Spielvogel Bates Worldwide (owned by Saatchi) lost the Milky Way account, although it kept other Mars brand accounts, in what was perceived as a disciplinary action after Saatchi had openly boasted about its high profits. "Mr. [Forrest Jr.] Mars thought that some of these profits came at his expense," explained one ad agency executive. After having made its point, Mars gave the agency several new assignments.

In early 1988, Mars held a 37 percent market share vs. Hershey's 36 percent. More important, although the market had grown only 2.3 percent, Hershey's share had grown 3.5 percent. To showcase its recent achievement, Hershey announced a $4.5 million renovation of Hershey's Chocolate World visitor's center. Not since Frank's days had the Mars company allowed consumers into its Chicago plant. Nor were guests invited into the candy plants in New Jersey, Pennsylvania, Georgia, Tennessee or Texas, although Forrest Sr. had started tours at the Ethel M plant in Nevada. Mars knew it needed to keep swinging hard at Hershey Foods to keep its slight edge in the $5 billion candy bar business.

*1. Ethel H. Mars, Frank's second wife, was an obstacle to Forrest Sr.'s ambitions.*

*2. Gallahadion, Ethel's 1940 Kentucky Derby Winner, paid 35-1.*

*3. Forrest E. Mars Sr. dancing with daughter Jackie Mars Vogel. Jackie would do anything to please her father.*

*4. Private Forrest E. Mars Jr. skipped basic training for the Army's business school.*

*5. The only known photograph of John F. Mars, from Yale University Year Book.*

*6. Forrest E. Mars Jr. from Yale University Year Book.*

*7. Mars, Inc. headquarters in McLean, Virginia. No sign identifies this $12 billion multinational corporation.*

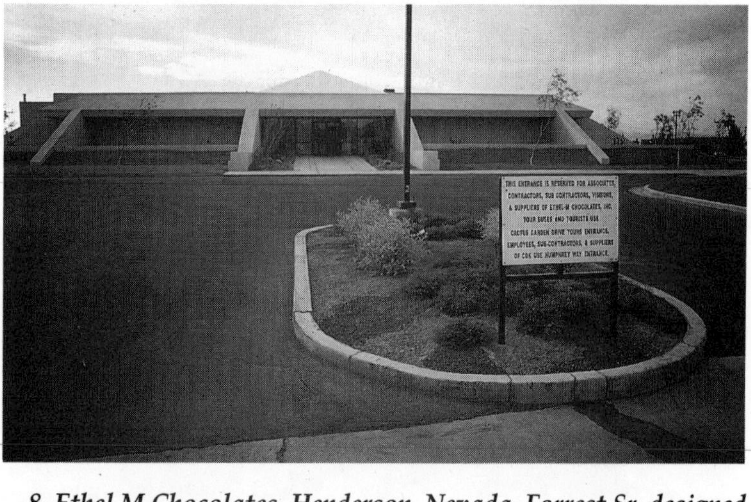


*8. Ethel M Chocolates, Henderson, Nevada. Forrest Sr. designed the bunker-like building.*

*9. Virginia Cretella Mars, recently divorced from Forrest Jr.*

*10. Audrey Meyer Mars (Mrs. Forrest E. Mars Sr.)*

*11. Marland, The Plains, Virginia, primary residence of the Mars family 1949-1992.*

*12. Residence of John and Adrienne Mars in McLean, Virginia, is worth $650,000.*

**13. *Hickory Corner, Bedminister, New Jersey, estate of Hank and Jackie Mars Vogel, estimated value $2 million.***

**14. *Stonehall Farm, The Plains, Virginia, estate of Jackie Mars Vogel, located a few miles from her childhood home, Marland.***

*15. Harold (Hank) A. Vogel Jr., "the bad, bad boy," according to Forrest Jr.*

*16. The Fourth Generation, daughters of Forrest Jr. and Virginia Mars. (From left: Pamela, Marijka, Valeria, Victoria.)*

# Five

# The Mars Meltdown

Mars was in orbit when it entered the 80s, having deposed Hershey Foods as the market share leader in 1970 and having increased its lead by 14 percentage points by 1979. "It took the Hershey people seven or eight years to realize that Mars was not going to go away," said one industry executive. "Then it took them another five years to get their act together."

The Pennsylvania company turned on the heat through new product development, aggressive marketing and fresh advertising strategies. Hershey's Kisses, for example, tripled in sales between 1977 and 1984. By the mid-80s, Mars finally began to melt under Hershey's fire.

Between them both, Hershey and Mars produced all of the country's top ten candy bars, five apiece. Together, the two companies possessed 70 percent of the industry's market share. Nestlé trailed behind.

But Hershey had a decided advantage over Mars because it sold 17 of the 60 best-selling candy bars. Mars only had nine of the top 60 bars. More important, few of the popular Mars candy bars were new products. Instead, the company was relying on the tried-and-true Snickers bar, M&Ms Plain and Peanut Candies, Milky Way and 3 Musketeers bars: all mature brands. Mars had developed no new candy products between 1977 and 1985. On the other hand, 20 percent of

Hershey candy sales in 1984 had come from its new products.

The only new Mars introductions that had panned out were the Twix Cookie Bars and Skittles candies, both introduced in 1976. However, even the Twix sales had gone flat by the end of 1988 and several other brands were doing very poorly. Balisto, a cereal bar, was eventually dropped. A recent launch, PB Max Real Peanut Butter Snack—a peanut butter chocolate bar—was intended to go against Hershey's Reese's Peanut Butter Cups, the number two candy behind Snickers in 1989. This, too, was a round that Hershey won hands down.

Among the new brands of Hershey that were rocketing along were its Big Block bars and premium Golden brand candies that appealed to more sophisticated tastes. Hershey, of course, had also entered the snack food arenas before Mars, and was a winner in the pasta business, which Mars had not entered at all.

At the same time, sales of such Mars brands as Snickers and Twix were level, or were slipping, as were Milky Way and 3 Musketeers. Even the M&M's brand looked like it was losing altitude.

Due to the brothers' disinclination to take risks, the company shied from developing new brands. John articulated the company's philosophy when he pointed out that most new products fail: given that, he said, his strategy was not to develop any new products! The brothers' peculiar logic and their unwillingness to take a chance translated for years into a total absence of new launches.

With 750 candy bar brands sold in the United States, the market was heavily saturated. It was difficult, but possible, to bring out a new brand, Forrest reminded his sons: Nestlé had done it with the Alpine bar, and Hershey with Bar None and others.

Mars, on the other hand, was merely repackaging, restyling and reformulating its brands. This approach was compensatory, at best, and the company knew it.

The great hope Mars associates had for DoveBars was dashed because of the nature of the small, competitive high-priced ice cream bar market. Much energy was focused on a product that, at best, would gain a small market share. Yet Mars did grab most of the novelty bar business, even if that was a relatively small category compared to other ice cream categories.

Mars also developed ice cream versions of its candy bar brands such as Milky Way Ice Cream Bars. Cloning its familiar candy bars into ice cream bars extended the company's range at relatively low risk. (Nestlé was doing the same thing, turning its Butterfinger and Nestlé Quik into ice cream bars.)

In Europe, Mars was helped by its decision to build the continent's largest ice cream production line, which opened in France in 1989. That same year, the British market grew by one-third. Still, ice cream sales were competitive in England, as Mars was up against the successful Walls ice cream business, a subsidiary of the giant Anglo-Dutch Unilever.

Another headache in Europe was distribution. DoveBars were hurt by retailers' exclusive contracts with Unilever. In a number of European countries, retailers are allowed to sell only Unilever products in the 50,000 freezers that Unilever supplies up and down the continent. Nor could Mars supply retailers with freezers of its own: retailers were forbidden from accepting them from other companies. This was particularly devastating to Mars as they were adding ice cream novelty bars to the company's line, with no place to sell them.

Mars sniffed, "Unilever's actions operate completely against a free market. It is hardly surprising that our sales have declined as we are excluded from about two-thirds of the retail outlets which could sell our brands."

Mars tried to get the Unilever agreements banned. A Unilever executive commented, "Mars could ruin the market for everyone. If it succeeds in getting our cabinets banned, a number of store owners will be forced to stop selling ice cream [because Unilever would remove the freezers and the retailers could not afford to replace them] so we will all end up suffering."

An industry analyst said of the new ice cream products that had nowhere to go, "Poor old Mars, it created a great idea but looks as though it has completely lost it."

Although Mars had bought DoveBar International ice cream, the only new candy company the brothers acquired was their father's tiny Ethel M Chocolates in 1988. Forrest Sr. was now in his mid-80s and growing less interested in running the firm he had founded a decade earlier. In fact, by this time his grandchildren were employed by Mars, Inc., including one—John's son Frank—who worked at Ethel M.

The Mars family was worried about their company's status, especially vis-a-vis Hershey. Forrest Jr. and John talked about involving Jackie in company business even though she had always been distant from its daily operations. Adding to the siblings' woes was that their father was dissatisfied with them. Forrest would rant at his sons and taunt them for their failure to develop new products, says a man close to the family.

What particularly bothered Forrest Sr. was the opportunity he saw his sons wasting. If he had been able to take control of the entire Mars candy operations as a young man, instead of having to wait until he was 60 years old, he could have made Mars into an entire galaxy of its own. But here were his sons, fumbling with the ball he had passed to them.

Mars associates knew to never mention Forrest to his sons. Just hearing his name made them cringe with insecurity.

The criticism from their father, coupled with the stress they felt from falling sales, made the brothers' mood ugly. Being number two did not sit well with them.

One former associate told *Fortune* magazine, "When market share is growing healthily, everything is okay, but when sales flatten out or even when goals are not quite met, guys can start tearing each other's throats out."

Unfortunately, the brothers often expressed their rivalry and divisiveness by choosing one another's staff members to scapegoat. When a problem came to the brothers' attention, Forrest Jr., for example, would pick out one of John's managers to blame. In his turn John, if he suspected an obstacle in one of Forrest Jr.'s divisions, would choose one of his brothers' associates as his victim. Managers felt that they were continually caught in the cross-fire between the two men.

The dismissal of Jones a few years earlier, the subsequent reassignment of executives and the fact that the company was starting to hire top staff from outside Mars, Inc. were all signs that the brothers were running scared. The company was getting further away from the one that their father had left them. Although it could not be considered exactly a bloated bureaucracy, it was not the lean organization Forrest Sr. had preferred, where line managers could take the responsibility to make their own decisions. Now, only a few managers working with the company's largest brands were allowed a say.

In addition, they had lost their quality edge: those standards that Forrest Sr. had introduced to the industry were now widespread. Other companies had caught up with Mars, and indeed were soon to surpass it.

Associates were even starting to complain that their pay was no longer significantly higher than others in the industry. The one factor that had made it worthwhile to put up with the brothers' mercurial ways was disappearing.

## Breakups

Against all odds, Forrest Sr. and Audrey celebrated their golden anniversary in 1980. The secret of their marriage's long survival seemed to be that they saw very little of each other. Forrest was still living above the Ethel M plant in Henderson, Nevada while Audrey was at the Watergate in Washington. When Forrest sold Ethel M at the end of the 80s, he began paying rent for his penthouse digs. The rent check went, of course, to Mars, Inc.

Forrest was amazed to find himself in his mid-80s and still healthy. As a young man, he never thought he would live beyond 50, the age his father died. Forrest's fear was illogical, for he refused to acknowledge that his mother had lived to nearly 100 and that his father's early death was probably the result of his having contracted polio as a boy, which had ruined his health.

But Frank's premature demise shadowed Forrest's life; years earlier, he had even turned most of his assets over to Audrey to lessen what he assumed would be the burden of his estate taxes on her. She would surely outlive him, he had thought. His unexpected longevity and Audrey's eventual diagnosis of cancer now made him suspect that his financial planning might not have been percipient.

Forrest and Audrey's children's marriages were not faring as well as the parental unit's. And one of those children was about to embark on an escapade that would cast some light into the darker corners of the Mars empire.

Daughter Jackie was restless and bored. She had done very little work for the Mars corporation even though she had been a board director since 1973 and received a salary. Instead, she left the role of active Mars associate to her husband, David Badger.

Jackie preferred a relatively quiet life as a well-off horsewoman in Potomac, Maryland. Her passion for riding brought her to buy a house with grounds that were more elaborate than those of her brothers. Her 10 acres on Three Sisters Road included a stable where she kept up to a half dozen horses. But as her children—Alexandra, Steven and Christa—grew older, she felt at odds with herself. Like many wealthy women, she seemed to lack a central core that gave her life meaning, and she kept waiting for other people in her life to bring her happiness. With that attitude, it was inevitable that she should blame her discontent on Badger.

Jackie met Harold A. Vogel, Jr. at the Washington International Horse Show in late fall of 1980. "Hank" was owner, with his brother Jack, of a well-known custom riding boot and shoe business called E. Vogel boots. The company was founded in 1879 by Hank's grandfather, Egidius, who had emigrated to New Jersey from Munich, Germany. Vogel boots are recognized as perhaps the world's most elegant and they have been worn by riders from Black Jack Pershing to Paul Newman. The company even produces boots for the United States Equestrian Team. It was natural for Jackie to select a boot of this quality for herself, for unlike her brothers and their wives, Jackie did not mind putting good money down for quality objects.

Hank was staffing the Vogel booth when the friendly-looking heavy-set woman with graying hair and dark eyes approached. They chatted as Hank measured her. Before she left, the Mars heiress paid for the $350 black French calf leather boots with a charge card that identified her simply as Jackie Badger.

At the time, Hank was in the process of a divorce from his first wife. He spent part of each year traveling to horse shows throughout the world as the representative of E. Vogel. Hank is so well-known to riders and to the company's retailers that he has been called "the face of E. Vogel." Hank worked the "outside" of E. Vogel while his brother remained "inside" the Manhattan office to run the daily operations of the business.

Hank's success as a salesman is not due only to the quality product he represents but also to his genuine warmth and interest in people. It was natural that a man like Hank would appeal to Jackie, coming as she does from a family that is cold and distant, yet controlling.

When Jackie was notified that her boots were ready, she insisted on picking them up herself rather than having them shipped, as is customary. She traveled to New York to get to the E. Vogel store, tucked into a hard-to-find neighborhood in lower Manhattan, between Little Italy, Soho and Chinatown.

Having made sure that Hank would be in the shop that day, Jackie struck up another friendly conversation. Soon, she disclosed to him that she and Badger were "estranged" and that she had not been happy for about ten years. She and Hank began meeting for lunch or dinner. They talked of their hopes for their children and the disappointments they had in their marriages.

Around April, Jackie called Hank excitedly. Badger was going to be out of town on business: would Hank escort her to a dance?

"Well," Hank thought, "you try to be nice to your customers but you don't necessarily want to date them."

Hank raised to Jackie the serious implications of this invitation but she persisted in urging him to join her. "I wasn't sure but I did go along. I needed to tread carefully."

In the end, fascination and a sense of adventure won out over caution: he decided to take her up on the invitation. From that point, they were together nearly every weekend. They even attended social events together, under the pretense of being "just friends."

Within a matter of months, Jackie and Hank felt deeply for each other. Jackie, when she wished, could be charming and almost carefree. Hank is an optimist who does his best to enjoy each day.

During this time, Hank still had not caught on to Jackie's maiden name nor her connection to the global candy company. He could tell that she had more money than he did, however, and comprehended that she was used to a glamorous lifestyle.

Meeting Hank seemed to spur Jackie to make up her mind to divorce Badger and, by the fall of 1981, Jackie and Hank were talking about marriage. But for at least a year after they first met, Jackie and Hank had been conducting a relationship that was kept secret from David Badger, her children and the rest of the Mars family.

Jackie filed for divorce from Badger in 1983 and she and Hank continued seeing each other and traveling together, although they were not living together. Jackie's divorce was made final in 1985. Badger continued working for the Mars company as he had done all his life, although he was reassigned from the headquarters office—and in one associate's wife's words— "banished to Hong Kong."

Jackie spent money more openly than she had before, as if her divorce had freed her from more than one constraint. Usually, said Hank, "she hated spending money. She counted every penny. I figured she was on an allowance from the family and that they didn't give her as much as she wanted."

As the couple plunged themselves into wedding plans, Jackie casually mentioned that Hank would have to sign a prenuptial agreement before they exchanged vows. She blamed her brothers for making her ask Hank to sign, saying that they insisted on it. Hank by now knew that Jackie was a Mars heir but did not realize the extent of her assets. For decades, the Mars company and the family had pursued a policy of secrecy and privacy, lowballing estimated sales figures and keeping their name out of the press.

With Hank, at least, their efforts succeeded.

## "Lucky Hank"

To be nearer Hank, Jackie bought a house in New Jersey. She chose the affluent horsey town of Bedminster, well known for its hunt. Another Jackie, this one named Onassis, also owned property in the area and rode in the hunt, held on Mondays, Wednesdays and Saturdays from late August to mid-February. In Middleburg, Virginia, the Orange County Hunt required a member to be a landowner, so Jackie Badger assumed that the Essex Fox Hounds hunt had a similar requirement. Although this turned out to be a misperception, Jackie had already become interested in a beautiful nineteenth-century farmhouse sited on 60 acres.

For her down payment on the $1.8 million Bedminster property located on River Road, she needed $200,000. Claiming she did not have the money, she borrowed it from Hank, further adding to his perception of her as being well-off but not fabulously wealthy.

By this time, Hank's friends knew that he was intending to marry a woman who was richer than he. "Lucky Hank," was the comment.

Occasionally, in the months before their marriage, Jackie would bring up the prenuptial agreement. Hank decided to defer to Jackie's wishes, and briefly conferred with an attorney. His own assets, including his share in E. Vogel Boots and real estate holdings, amounted to slightly less than a million dollars.

As the wedding day approached, Jackie asked Hank, "How do you feel about marrying a very wealthy woman?"

Hank asked, "What are we talking about?"

Jackie then disclosed that she had a net worth of "about $30 million." But any assets she had were tied up in trusts, she said.

Jackie and Hank set March 15, 1986 as their wedding date so that Christa could continue to attend the Potomac School, in McLean, Virginia, where Forrest and John's children had also gone to elementary school and where Forrest's wife had served on the board.

Hank was traveling a great deal in early 1986; so Jackie's lawyer drafted the prenuptial agreement that she and her family insisted upon, and sent the agreement to Hank's lawyer. Meantime, Jackie's attorney called Hank several times and on at least one occasion had lunch with him to urge him to sign the document.

Finally, on March 14, 1986, less than 24 hours before the wedding, the prenuptial agreement was presented to Hank and signed. Documents were attached showing certain holdings of Jackie's such as property and trust assets, including the Forrest Edward Mars Charitable Trust of 1959 and the Jacqueline Mars Badger Trust of 1975. However, there was no aggregate value given in the documents. The closest estimate Jackie had ever given of her wealth was the $30 million figure she had earlier mentioned to Hank.

The terms of the agreement cut Hank out of any rights to Jackie's assets in the case of either divorce or death. In part, it read: " . . . each of the parties hereby waives all rights he or she may have to and agrees to request that a court make no further provision for separate maintenance, . . . suit money, support, alimony or maintenance or any other form of payment, or any award or settlement of property or income of the other party . . . in connection with any such separation or termination or dissolution of their marriage, including legal fees. . . . "

Although these strictures might seem unduly stringent, Jackie repeatedly told Hank that there were Mars family reasons for her asking him to sign the prenuptial agreement. She also assured him that she would take care of him for the rest of his life, that she would make substantial transfers of monies to him and that she would protect him with significant amounts of life insurance.

The couple married in a quiet ceremony at the tony St. John's Episcopal Church in Alexandria, Virginia. The only guests in attendance were Hank's adult children, Dean and Elizabeth, and Jackie's children, Alexandra, 20, Steve, 17 and Christa, 11.

But the wedding bells took on a discordant note for Hank when he learned from Jackie that the newlyweds were to be accompanied on their honeymoon by one of Jackie's daughters, the daughter's girlfriend, and Jackie's son Steve. Hank objected to this connubial party of five, but not with as much disappointment as he felt, since he assumed there would be opportunities for romantic trips in the future. He also thought this would be a good opportunity to get to know Jackie's children and help them adjust to their mother's new marriage.

In the early days of their marriage Hank became aware that Jackie disliked being alone with anyone, ever. She was more comfortable in a group than with Hank. As time went on, they continued nearly always to take their vacations and trips with other people. And, at home, the constant presence of live-in help made Hank feel he was never allowed to be with his wife, unescorted.

One woman who knew Jackie sympathized with Hank's problems, saying, "No one can ever get really close to Jackie."

Hank learned to tolerate what originally were merely irritations in their marriage because any attempt to discuss problems made Jackie go ballistic. For example, one of Hank's sisters is a successful interior designer who visited the Bedminster house to help Jackie with its decoration. It was not long before the designer suggested to Jackie that one of her choices might not be aesthetically pleasing. Jackie was furious, and told Hank that she did not want anything more to do with his sister. Worse still, she was angry at Hank for refusing to take sides.

Hank's family and friends learned to put up with Jackie, her moods and her changes of mind. Once, Jackie and Hank and their combined families were to take a trip to Bermuda. But Jackie got mad about something and, at the last minute, refused to go. So the group went without her.

If Jackie and Hank's home life seemed less than idyllic, storm clouds were also gathering over the Mars headquarters in McLean.

## Hershey Pulls Ahead

In a fast, aggressive move in August of 1988, Hershey acquired the United States division of Cadbury Schweppes as a franchise for $270 million in cash and $30 million in debt. The company used cash from its sale of the Friendly's restaurant chain, selling the chain because, as Hershey Chairman and Chief Executive Officer Ken Wolfe said, "It was a totally different business from our others and we didn't have the management capacity to add value to the operation."

Through its buy of Cadbury Schweppes' American confectionery operation, Hershey added the familiar and popular York Peppermint Patties, Mounds and Almond Joy brands to Hershey's roster. The latter two candies were then the fifteenth and sixteenth most popular in the United States. The company also bought the smaller Reading-based Dietrich Corporation, the maker of 5th Avenue candy bars, Ludens throat drops and Queen Anne chocolate-covered cherries.

Through these acquisitions, Hershey increased its share of the United States market to 44 percent, well ahead of Mars' 37 percent. Also, Hershey's well-known pasta brands, including Ronzoni and San Giorgio, put it in second place in that market, behind Borden. (The company had added pasta products in 1966 in order to lessen its reliance on chocolate.)

Sources within the industry said that Forrest Jr. and John were "annoyed" at Hershey's acquisition of Cadbury; sweating blood was more like it. For within the Mars company and within the family, the brothers were gloomy and tense, especially as other mergers and acquisitions by such companies as Nestlé and Jacobs Suchard headlined the business pages. Jacobs Suchard bought E.J. Brach & Sons of Chicago, while Nestle's purchase of Rowntree brought its market share nearly to the level of Mars.

Nestlé's dominant size also cast a shadow over the European operations of Mars. By buying the popular English candy firm Rowntree and picking up such popular brands as Kit Kat, Nestlé increased its share in the British market to 24 percent. Nestlé's strategic plan was to bring the Rowntree candies to the continent, where they would further threaten the stability of the European kingdom of Mars.

Mars, unlike the other candy giants, refused to buy any new concerns. Its fear of long-term debt had become as strong as its aversion to publicity. Rather than gaining on other companies through acquiring new brands, Mars focused on bringing candy that was popular in one part of the world to another. It introduced its Bounty candy bar to the United States from overseas, where it had been popular for more than a decade as the U.K.'s fourth best-selling Mars brand and the country's top coconut bar.

Although many believed that this was its American introduction, Bounty had actually been test marketed in the 70s and failed. Its hasty, unplanned introduction to a national American market in January 1989, only four months after Hershey took away Mars' crown, was intended to compete directly with Hershey's newly acquired Mounds and Almond Joy coconut bars. Mars' move was called a copycat technique that would be unsuccessful, as knockoffs usually fail in their attempt to beat the leader in a candy category. Critics again pointed out that Mars was unable to compete against the innovations of Hershey.

Since Mars was not acquiring companies or developing new products, it needed to extend its candy bar lines through manufacturing variations on its most popular brands. In April, 1989, Mars revived its Forever Yours bar that had been taken off the market 10 years earlier due to sagging sales. Forever Yours had been a similar candy to Milky Way, varying only in its nougat being vanilla rather than chocolate, and in its coating being dark rather than milk chocolate. Mars renamed the bar Milky Way Dark: since Milky Way was the fifth most popular bar, the company felt that associating the new bar with the Milky Way brand would give it a popularity boost. It also hoped that the aging baby boomers would be ready for the dark chocolate taste.

As Mars' strategy was to go with the tried and true, and develop line extensions rather than new products, it unveiled its first variation on Snickers, the country's most popular candy bar, in early 1990. Peanut Butter Snickers leveraged brand equity by capitalizing on the country's top-selling candy bar.

Although in the past Mars had played down the Mars name on its candy bars and had advertised its brands separately, now it grouped three of the bars—Mars, Milky Way and Milky Way Dark—in what appeared to be a corporate image spot. Mars hoped that its "Making life a little sweeter—Mars" theme would soon become as familiar as Chevrolet's "Heartbeat of America."

In fact, Mars was looking for advertising co-sponsors to help market its products. As the competition heightened, the insulated Mars was trying to think creatively. One idea was to link up with Walt Disney Co. so that familiar Disney characters—including Mickey Mouse, who was soon to celebrate his sixtieth birthday—could be shown in Mars candy advertisements.

"I don't think the days of new products are over," said a Mars spokesman, "but it's very costly to develop a new product. You'd better make sure you don't fall on your face."

That statement proved to be prophetic, because in March 1989 Mars announced the production of Sussande, a line of fine chocolates that were positioned to appeal to adult palates. Its upscale ingredients of toffee, caramel and pralines, it was hoped, would entice sophisticated taste buds. But once again, Mars lagged behind Hershey, which six months earlier had introduced Symphony chocolate bar—a creamy, smooth chocolate bar that also has a toffee-praline version. Symphony already ranked in the top 20 candy bars during its test marketing. Both Hershey's Symphony and Mars' Sussande were those companies' adjustments to a new population profile composed of older, more affluent customers.

However, Sussande's price of $1.40 a bar was too high to win over even these more well-heeled consumers. The Mars superpremium bar failed miserably, costing the company an estimated $100 million.

Mars did, though, score a major coup when it debuted a M&M's Peanut Butter Chocolate Candies to compete against Hershey's Reese's Pieces. Some Mars insiders had feared that the candy would cannibalize sales of M&M's Plain and Peanut. But since the M&M's Peanut Butter included chocolate, prevailing wisdom held that it would have more potential to beat Hershey's brand than Bounty had over Mounds and Almond Joy, or than Summit, its chocolate-wafer brand that failed to overtake the bar it had imitated, Hershey's Kit Kat.

Ironically, some industry analysts feel that Mars should have stayed with Summit, and would have done so if the brothers had not insisted in being number one all the time. Summit was doing well as a niche bar with $40 million in sales, they note, and it was killed only because it wasn't a blockbuster. The company believes in maximum asset utilization, or, as reporter Bill Saporito termed it in *Fortune* magazine, "beating its plants to death."

Yet in an $8.7 billion market, not all niches are small. Tootsie Roll Industries, for example, producers of Tootsie Rolls, Charms, Mason Dots and other candies, has a traditional market niche as the world's largest producer of lollipops and was outdoing its previous sales each quarter. President Ellen Gordon points out that Tootsie Roll Industry's strength in the candy market comes, in part, from its being a niche player. "We have a particular niche where we control the market. We have Junior Mints, Tootsie Rolls, Tootsie Pops and Charleston Chews, among other candies.

No one else can make these or have the brand equity to do so."

Additionally, the Tootsie company is in the right place at the right time: "We have very low fat candy," notes Gordon. "Tootsie Pops have no fat. Tootsie Rolls are low in fat and are on many heart diets. Junior Mints are low in fat and Mason Dots have no fat. We are in the right ballpark for people who want low fat candies."

The Gordon family's goals for the company, she says, is to "continue to make greater quantities of high quality candy under our brand names by introducing new products and to grow profitably through these introductions and through our extensions. And also to grow through acquisitions."

Acquisitions have never been a Mars forte. And the Mars brothers' killer insistence on always being number one works against them in a market where other companies have profitably learned to be niche players.

The brothers finally had the fire lit under them when Hershey's regained the lead. Everyone was watching to see the direction they would follow. The president of Leaf Inc., maker of Milk Duds candies, commenting on Mars, said, "Their current marketing theory is to throw everything against the wall and see if something sticks."

Since candy eaters usually choose a different candy bar each time they make a purchase, it is important for a company to have a variety of bars in front of the consumer. At least Mars finally seemed to be waking up to the realization that it needed to produce more products, even if they were line extensions like Milky Way Dark or M&M's Peanut Butter Chocolate Candies. New flavors of Kudos, Starburst and Skittles were also introduced.

Hershey had been putting a greater variety of candy bars in front of the consumer years before the slow-learner Mars caught on. As Hershey's candy bars became the nation's most popular, the company's distribution muscle waxed stronger. Mars was beginning to realize that it needed to improve its treatment of candy distributors, who had never been of great concern to the company before. One of them pointed out, "When you are No. 1, people need you. When you are No. 2, trying to be No. 1, you need everyone."

The second jolt felt by Mars at the end of the 80s was when Nestlé passed Mars as the world's largest candy producer. Nestlé has been called the most multinational of all global companies because only two percent of its sales are made in Switzerland, its home country.

When the world's largest food company overtook Mars in 1989, Mars realized that it might not be able to regain its lead position in either the United States or in the world marketplace.

## Cat Fights

Early in 1989, confused pet owners searched grocery store aisles in vain for their familiar Kal Kan cat food, manufactured by a Mars division. Kal Kan, which had been a feline staple for 20 years, was no longer on the shelves. Instead, shoppers spotted similar-looking cans of a different brand. If they read the small print, they could find the words Kal Kan on the label, but it was overshadowed by the new brand name: Whiskas.

Before it was abruptly dropped by Mars, Kal Kan had been the country's second most popular canned cat food, with sales of $250 million that ranked the brand slightly below Star-Kist 9 Lives. (Finicky spokescat Morris had made Star-Kist the market share leader.) Other pet food businesses that fell behind the Mars brands are Ralston-Purina, H.J. Heinz, Carnation and Quaker Oats. Although Whiskas was unknown to United States shoppers, it was Mars' best-selling cat food worldwide, having nearly one billion dollars in sales in Europe, Japan, Canada and Australia. The recipes for Kal Kan and Whiskas were virtually identical.

This was not the first time Mars had changed the brand name. In 1987, in partial response to a shrinking dog food market—beginning in 1984, low-maintenance cats had begun to outrank canines in double-income household popularity—Mars changed the name of Kal Kan canned dog food to Pedigree, and changed the name of Mealtime dry dog food to Pedigree Mealtime. Experimenting with brand equity worked in that case: in one year, Pedigree gained a slight lead over Grand Metropolitan's Alpo brand, reversing their traditional ranks.

Mars wished to market its products and product images globally, emulating Coca-Cola's style. The brothers were willing to chance replacing the Kal Kan brand with Whiskas to help the company develop a stronger brand image. Although Forrest Jr. and John agreed to the change, they could not take credit for the idea. The switch was pushed into place by a bright young manager named Al Poe who noted that the Kal Kan line of dog and cat food controlled only seven percent of the market and was starting to soften.

Additionally, the company preferred to deal with as few advertising companies as possible and hoped that a unified cat food brand would let it consolidate advertising and marketing campaigns in the same way that major international brands could do. Finally, focus group tests showed that the Whiskas name had a far better image with cat owners than Kal Kan and that, since cat owners bond tightly with their pets, a name with a warmer connotation would be appealing.

The sort of global branding aspired to at Mars was thumpingly rejected by Nestlé. That multinational corporation prefers to keep its brands local, reflecting the culture of the country in which they are sold.

Before long, an intense campaign that doubled advertising dollars had introduced cat owners to the Whiskas name. Promotions were so costly that it seemed the firm was giving the product away to gain share, a move usually antithetical to Mars philosophy and practice. Yet the company's market share had doubled to 14 percent within two years.

Some still questioned the wisdom of trying to go global with a product in this category. It might work with candy bars, they thought, but it would not succeed in the cat food arena. As one industry expert said, "When it comes right down to it, how can you market cat food worldwide when in some countries cats *are* food?"

# Six

# Shifts In The Family Constellation

Two years that were difficult for the Mars family, for both business and personal reasons, were 1988 and 1989. First, and worst, Audrey was dying of cancer. The woman who had spent thousands of volunteer hours for the American Cancer Society—and who had recently underwrote a generously endowed professorship called the Audrey Meyer Mars Professorship in Geriatric Research at The Medical College of Pennsylvania—succumbed to that disease in June 1989. At her bedside was her beloved maid of 35 years, Mary, who remained in the family's employ.

Since Forrest, thinking that he would die first, had transferred considerable assets to his wife, it was assumed that Audrey's will would be equally generous. But she had never forgiven him for an earlier affair, one that he thought was long forgotten. At her death, Forrest learned his wife of 59 years had left him a "spendthrift trust" so that he would be prohibited from having total access to the money that he had earned and already gifted to her. In essence, Forrest now receives an allowance from his wife's estate.

"I should have divorced her," Forrest bitterly told others at the time.

There were other lesser, but still disturbing, troubles during those two years for the Mars family. Not only had their company been knocked out of the lead by Hershey but Forrest Jr. was divorcing Virginia, with possible implications for the stability of the company. If either of the brothers had the time to start a romantic relationship while married and running a company, it would have been Forrest. He had always been less work-driven than his younger brother John, and made sure to take time off each year to deep-sea fish or ski. True to type, Forrest Jr. had started a relationship with a Mars associate, Deborah Adair Clarke, who worked in the company's snack food division as a mere zone five employee (as one nose-out-of-joint associate sniffed). The smitten Forrest was determined to divorce the well-liked Ginny, the mother of his four adult daughters—who were working for the Mars companies.

Naturally, Forrest Jr. and Deborah's romance became an item for whispered discussion among the associates, many of whom could not understand what this woman in her 30s saw in him. People were also talking about how the divorce might even force a partial breakup of the Mars company in order for Virginia to obtain a fair settlement from her husband.

Virginia, of course, suffered when she learned that Forrest was leaving her. She is a reserved, discreet and circumspect woman who remained loyal to the Mars code of secrecy even while she was in pain from her husband's actions. Like her mother-in-law's, her activities had centered around philanthropy, including support for Washington's National Symphony Orchestra. But her public positions were of the unimpeachable lady-of-the-manor sort; she never aired dirty laundry in public. She is also characterized as being a truly kind person. So even though she was embarrassed by the situation Forrest placed her in, she did not talk about her painful feelings with outsiders.

Within the family, however, Virginia made it clear that she was a force to be reckoned with. And so, rather than have her challenge the amount of her settlement, possibly forcing Forrest to make information about the company available to her, Forrest agreed to pay Virginia $50 million and give her, among other assets, deeds to their three houses, including her residence on Belgrove Road and a modest ski chalet they owned in Austria. The divorce became final in January, 1990 and Forrie Mars saw to it that the divorce papers were sealed by judicial order.

John was the only one of the siblings who remained in his original marriage. He concentrated his energies on the company. By now, it had become apparent that Forrest Jr., who wanted to spend even more leisure hours with his younger wife, was focusing on his personal life. He could increasingly be found at the posh Weslie apartment building they lived in at 1401 N. Oak Street in Rosslyn, overlooking the famous Iwo Jima sculpture on the bank of the Potomac River. He also looked forward to visiting the lush estate they bought on one of the Leeland Islands of the Caribbean called Montserrat—which has no commercial flights, keeping out those who cannot afford a private air charter. Forrest scuba dives and fishes in his leisure time, and it seemed that he would retire before he was 70, and allow John to take over the company.

John's only passion outside the company was flying. He earned a pilot's license when he was in Australia as a young man but would never fly in the United States. After all, a man who did not take risks would not pilot a plane in America's crowded, unsafe skies. Only when he could visit a Mars office in Australia would he take the helm of a plane.

Flying seems to be one of the few non-Mars topics that can light up John's personality. One nervous manager had to meet John for dinner outside of Reading, England at a low-cost English restaurant John had chosen. "The evening was not going very well as John didn't seem to be interested in anything I had to say," remembered the associate.

"Then the conversation drifted onto air travel, which seemed to spark his interest. For the next 20 minutes, he bombarded me with his intimate knowledge of the world's international flight schedules."

## Jackie and Hank

For years, all Mars profits were reinvested back into the company. Forrest and John drew good salaries, but none of the three siblings received dividends until the 80s. Still, even dividends were not enough to meet the financial demands of Forrest Jr.'s divorce. Assets would have to be accessed.

Thus, the combination of Audrey's death and Forrest Jr.'s need for cash for his divorce settlement with Virginia, brought an influx of money to Forrest Jr., John and Jackie that amounted to $75 million—in cash—to each sibling for redemption of stock. (Of course, after taxes this came to a mere $47 million for each Mars sibling.) This flood of money marked the beginning of the end of Jackie's marriage.

Shortly after Jackie received this huge amount of cash, the financial duping of Hank took a new turn when Jackie told him that she needed to file a separate federal tax return for 1990. Hank was puzzled, as this was the first time the couple would not file jointly. She alleged that Forrest and John were unhappy that Hank's tax return time needed to be extended, since Hank had not received all the interest statements from his investments. Therefore, for the first time in the marriage, Jackie's brothers wanted her to file a separate tax return.

In mid-1991, the treasurer of Mars, Vito Spitaleri, sent Jackie a note that read: "Your 1991 and subsequent tax returns will be filed separately—not jointly with Hank—and will be handled and filed by McLean. All copies will be maintained here."

(Spitaleri seems intimately involved with the Mars family's private finances, in addition to his formal role as treasurer of the company. Even simple household repairs or renovations require a personal okay from Spitaleri before workmen can proceed.)

As Hank later testified, the Spitaleri memorandum elaborated on its implication that the redemption of stock for $75 million would be disguised from him. The note continues: "Transfers from accounts in McLean will be handled by Rita as is done for transfers of current dividends to your operating accounts so that the appearance will be maintained of regular transfers as needed without any apparent change in source."

As Hank later realized, what was happening was that he was not going to be told about his wife's new influx of $75 million. The money would be kept in Virginia, not in New Jersey where the couple lived. In addition, by Hank's being kept from filing a joint return with his wife, he would have no idea that she had come into an incredible financial windfall.

Of course, at the time he had little idea of what was going on. What he did recognize was the extent of his brothers-in-law's concerns about the future of the Mars company, because they insisted that Jackie had to help them out. "If you're going to own a third of the company," her brothers told her, "we want you back here, working like us."

At the time that Jackie married Hank, she had played no role in the company's daily management. Though she drew a salary, she did not act like an employee as she did not report to work, nor did she seem to have any specific job duties—although she did have a designated metal desk, facing a back wall in the corner of headquarters' second floor.

Jackie had traveled for the firm but it had always been kept to a minimum. At the time of their marriage, the understanding Hank had was that any further involvement and travel would take no more of Jackie's time then it had in the past. Jackie told Hank that her brothers' management style at work was "brutal" and that she did not care to be a part of it.

Now, Forrest and John were running scared. They needed any help they could get to assist Mars to ascend to its rightful place at the top of the candy industry. And since the Marses trust few people outside the family, it was natural for Forrie and John to turn to Jackie.

Then, too, they had already antagonized their managers too often. Even the two brothers realized that neither man was the right Mars to rally the associates and win the battles underway against Hershey and Nestlé. So, says Hank, they turned to the more personable Jackie to be the liaison between the brothers and the various Mars executives. Perhaps she would be liked and respected by the top associates. They conferred upon her the title of corporate vice president in 1990.

The change meant a tremendous amount of traveling for Jackie, who was still raising a teenage daughter, Christa, who boarded at Holton Arms School back in Potomac, Maryland. Jackie was gone for extended periods of time, and she did not take her husband with her on these business trips.

Jackie's new schedule placed additional strains on her marriage, as their understanding had been for Hank to cut down on the traveling he did for E. Vogel company. So now, Hank had reduced his load but Jackie was always flying to some foreign country. Rather than relying on her passive income from the company as she had for years, she became intensely involved with the activities of the Mars corporation. Hank began to think that, finally, the Mars company had gotten to Jackie and it was now the most important part of her life, just as it had been to her father and her brothers. Hank had never understood why the men wanted to run a worldwide empire as if it were a hands-on business; now his wife was insisting on having a finger in every pie. It was also obvious to Hank that Jackie had lost interest in their relationship.

One time Hank griped to one of the McLean top associates about the wear and tear the business was wreaking on his wife. Jackie was clearly enervated from her constant trips and Hank could not fathom why such a sophisticated and wealthy company had to micromanage their business so obsessively. Hank asked the executive, "Why do the brothers insist on handling everything in person? Can't they hold any of their meetings through teleconferences like other global companies?"

The associate gave Hank a level look and replied, "Because then they wouldn't be able to see the blood on the floor."

## China Blues

Forrest and John were still committed to global expansion as a means of growth for the company. Taking mature brands into new countries was less risky than developing new products and did not involve long-term debt, as could acquisitions. It was only natural that, after their early experiences with China's friendship stores (foreign currency shops), they would position their brands for the attention of a country with a population of a billion. Through the friendship stores and others, M&M's candies had become the second most popular western import to China, second only to cigarettes. In 1990, Mars was one of only a dozen foreign sponsors of the fall's 11th Asian Games in Beijing, and the number of retailers stocking M&M's doubled to 1,000 during its marketing blitz.

Of course, many other United States companies chose to pull out of China after the brutal 1989 suppression of the country's pro-democratic movement. After the political crackdown, few foreign businesses were interested in having a high profile in China because they did not want to be associated with China's hard-line regime. The firms also refused to sponsor the Asian Games. Mars quietly undertook an assessment of whether their support would harm their image in other Asian countries. Concluding that it would not, the company maintained its sponsorship.

Its action was not without risk. In September, 1990, an anonymous letter arrived at a Mars office in Hong Kong warning that, in protest of Mars' support of the games, a bag of M&M's candies in that country had been poisoned with sodium cyanide. The letter condemned the Beijing government for its repression of dissent and also denounced Mars for its support of the Asian Games, which, it charged, was tantamount to supporting the repressive Chinese government. Just as they had in England six years earlier, the company acted swiftly to pull hundreds of thousands of M&M's bags off supermarket shelves. Because M&M's sold in Hong Kong were exported from the company's Australian manufacturing plant, the bags were returned there to check for tampering.

No poisoned packets were found and Mars continued its support of the games, which was intended to bring the Chinese to greater brand awareness of M&M's. Flags decorated with the M&M's logo appeared along with official Asian Games flags on each lamppost for the 45-minute drive from the airport to Beijing. Just in case someone had missed seeing the ubiquitous flags, hot air balloons, large yellow tents and give-away umbrellas were all decorated with the M&M's logo.

At the opening ceremonies, as the military band played China's national anthem, a bright yellow M&M's balloon popped up over the tightly-packed Worker's Stadium. The Chinese leaders were furious and signaled for the balloon to be pulled down. It was: but not before stadium spectators and television audiences throughout China and Asia had seen it.

Mars had next to no competition from other western candy companies in China. Although Nestlé and Cadbury products were sold in large hotels and other foreign-currency outlets, supermarkets and mom-and-pop retail stores stocked only M&M's. The candy was still a luxury for the Chinese, however, due to its price. One motivation for opening a M&M's plant in China would be so that it would not have to be imported from Australia, cutting costs down. The head of the distribution company for M&M's guessed that it still might take 20 or 30 years for Mars to make a profit in China.

Showing that Mars was in it for the long haul, he commented, "There's a conscious decision to develop the brand in China. If it takes 50 years, that's okay."

## Candy's Good for You?

Sponsorship of the Asian games typified Mars' carefully crafted linkage between candy and athletes. As a reaction to the health-conscious era of the 70s, when sugar consumption dropped by 20 percent per person from 1968 to 1975, Mars had started a campaign to promote the putative health benefits of its products.

As early as 1969, the company's television advertisement for Milky Way bars showed a glass of milk magically changing into a Milky Way candy bar. The ad clearly implied that the candy bar's nutritional value is equivalent to that of a glass of milk, and that the candy bar could be substituted for milk or milk products because the company uses these as ingredients. The advertisement caught the attention of the Federal Trade Commission, which issued a provisional consent order barring Mars from so misrepresenting the dietary advantages of Milky Way bars. The company withdrew the ads.

But later that decade, Action for Children's Television continued to protest to the FTC that misleading nutritional information was still given out in Mars' ads. Mars was by then pushing for an association between candy bars and such other snack foods as pretzels and cookies, which either contained no sugar or had a sugar content lower in proportion to other ingredients than that found in candy. At the beginning of the 80s, the company was putting a "Now Foods" campaign into place. According to a Mars manager, the message was aimed at people who incorrectly feel "that if something tastes good it can't be good for you."

The company published a brochure with the message that "since snacking is now integral to our eating habits, snack foods should be nutritionally sound as well as fun to eat. . . Snack foods containing chocolate, milk, nuts and sugar provide some of these essential nutrients." Additionally, Mars began adding nutritional labeling—which was not required at that point—to show the candy's theoretical food value.

"I would not recommend a steady diet of nothing but Snickers bars," said a Mars official in a speech to the candy industry, "nor would I recommend a steady diet of nothing but sirloin steak, but I would recommend the occasional consumption of either or both as components of a pleasurable, balanced diet pattern."

Over the years, various Mars spokesmen continue to hammer at this point, saying that some of the candy's ingredients—notably, milk and peanuts—are nutritious and "a legitimate part of a balanced diet. We don't claim you can live on Snickers, but you can't live on apples or bananas, either." If you wonder why Snickers is frequently mentioned by the company, it's because that bar's peanuts give it a higher protein value than many other candy products.

As the company attempted to have the public perceive candy as a good snack that happens to be sweet rather than as junk food, it made the sponsorship of athletes part of its mission. So it was that in 1984, Mars paid $5 million to name M&M's and Snickers the official snack foods of the 1984 Olympics. The Mars spokesman said, "With the Olympics, we saw a chance to enhance our nutritional message and tell people they did not have to be closet eaters of our products."

An irony was that even though Mars was trying to position its products as wholesome snacks, it was still slow to expand into such related health-food fields as granola bars.

Its integrity was even questioned when it did finally promote granola products. After the Kudos bars had been on the market a few years, they began to sport a new claim on their labels: "Lower in fat than ever." Of course, the bar was lower in fat—because it had been downsized. And it still had more fat than other leading granola bars. A Mars spokesman denied any impropriety and said, "In no way are we misleading the consumers."

But an attempt by Mars to "educate" the public about the "significant nutrient values" of M&M's Peanut led to media derision after Mars' president for "scientific affairs" noted that both kinds of M&Ms, plain and peanut, "surpass apples in protein, calcium, zinc, iron and other nutrients."

One columnist responded, "The man from Mars left out the negatives. M&M's are high in sugar and fat, with one rotting teeth and the other clogging arteries."

Protests against the nutritional claims being made by Mars were being heard in the United Kingdom, too. An English group called Action and Information on Sugars unsuccessfully complained to that country's television commission because Milky Ways were touted to children as "The sweet you can eat between meals without ruining your appetite." The health lobbyist group charged that Mars was in violation of England's strict rules prohibiting ads that encourage children to snack frequently throughout the day. Although the complaint was rejected, Mars subsequently changed its telly advertisement to the innocuous, "It's the good taste that's in Milky Way."

Still, candy industry lobbyists such as Mark Andrews, former United States Senator from Nebraska, remain eager to put forward the argument that chocolate is "a healthy snack," citing its use by the military as a fast source of high-energy food. In New York state, other candy industry lobbyists tried to overturn a 1987 law that prohibited selling candy to children in public schools before lunch. Summing up their message, Andrews criticizes "the nutrition faddists that are out there who continue to say that somehow or other chocolate is just not a nutritious snack."

By 1990, Mars announced it would be a sponsor of the 1992 Winter and Summer Olympics, again linking candy with an image of health and vitality. Since Mars continued making carefully crafted nutritional claims for its candy bars, it is not surprising that it soon got itself into a brouhaha over a related issue, tooth decay.

## Spin Dentistry

In England, Mars donated research money to the national General Dental Council for research on candy, chocolate and tooth decay in 1978. The Council "reluctantly" agreed to funds for research projects, saying it wished the money came from elsewhere but that it was given "entirely and absolutely without strings."

A different situation occurred in the United States in 1990, when dentists began receiving newsletters from the "Princeton Dental Resource Center" that contained articles and reports on dental health. The Princeton Center suggested that these newsletters be left in patient waiting rooms. Raffles for free trips were open to subscribers.

Two years later, some angry dentists charged that they had been misled. What aroused their ire was the unexpected advice they read in the Princeton newsletter that eating a chocolate bar regularly "might even inhibit cavities." That statement was spin dentistry, based on a UCLA study that tannins, contained in cocoa and other products, inhibit plaque formation. The associate professor of oral biology who headed the project said that his research was directed at isolating tannins from cocoa and other foods to be used as additives in toothpaste and mouthwash and that his work had been mischaracterized by the newsletter.

"Any gains you might get from the cocoa in chocolate would be more than offset by ingredients like sugar," he explained, since dental caries are started when sugars left by food are converted to acids that eventually cause cavities.

When it came out that Mars, Inc. had funded the Princeton Dental Center—which, egregiously, had no link with Princeton University and was merely located in Princeton, New Jersey—dentists, researchers and consumer groups were furious at having been bamboozled.

The director of the well-known Washington, D.C. consumer advocacy group, Center for Science in the Public Interest, said it was "the most brazen way of doing things that I have ever heard of."

The reaction at Mars was all innocence. Despite its deliberately misleading name, the Mars spokesman said that Mars' connection to the Center and its newsletter had not been a secret. On the other hand, no mention of the company's sponsorship was ever included in the newsletter, though Mars had funded at least 90 percent of the Princeton Dental Center, to the tune of around $1.5 million annually. Additionally, three Mars officials, along with several dentists, reviewed newsletter articles before publication.

Again, Mars brought down a storm of criticism on itself in several urban newspapers, including *The New York Times* and the *Chicago Tribune,* which poked fun at the company on their editorial pages.

The Attorney General of New York did not find the controversy amusing, however, and fined the Princeton Dental Center $25,000 for its sleight-of-hand in skewing information. Among the specific instances of misinformation cited by the Attorney General was Princeton Dental Center's claim that chocolate and caramel produced fewer cavities than such starches as bread or crackers.

Despite this official rebuke, Mars continues to confuse public policy makers. In 1995, the current Mars lobbyist, Mark Andrews, stated: "There are tests that show, and they've been repeated a number of times, that dental caries are caused by carbohydrates, not by sugar." He continued, "Sugar is a carbohydrate but if you eat a soda cracker before you go to bed at night it will be worse for your teeth than if you eat a caramel.

"A caramel is a self-cleaning type thing that doesn't stick to the teeth as much as a soda cracker would or a piece of bread."

This logic sounds remarkably like the "research findings" published by the Princeton Dental Center. The American Dental Association's spokesman Chris Martin snickered at Andrews' statement and explained that both sugar and carbohydrates, which break down into sugar, will cause dental caries. No study that Martin knew of has compared cavities that may develop after eating caramels with cavities that develop after eating bread or a soda cracker.

At the statement that caramels are self-cleaning, the ADA spokesman merely laughed and said, "I know who he's working for."

## Regaining the Number One Spot

After concern through the 70s of fat and sugar intake, Americans increased the amount of candy they ate in the 80s. Mars and other candy manufacturers were hopeful when they saw Americans consumption of candy was rising significantly: Americans ate nearly 21 pounds of candy in 1990, more than they had ever eaten before.

But in early 1991, in an attempt to accelerate revenues further, Hershey raised prices by a nickel a bar.

By four in the afternoon on that same day, Mars raised its prices identically.

The two companies, Mars and Hershey, formed "one of the strongest distribution oligopolies in the United States," according to *Forbes* magazine in 1992. Finding distributors and shelf space is difficult for candy outsiders; even Nestlé, a giant global corporation with ten percent of the United States market, was having a tough time competing against the two behemoths.

Consumers scaled back candy bar purchases after Hershey and Mars raised prices within hours of each other. But this cutback was insignificant to Mars compared to the good news it received later in the year: Mars reversed its position over Hershey, going up to nearly 18 percent of the market share while Hershey remained flat at 17 percent. M&M's Peanut Butter Chocolate Candies was a first-rate success: not only did consumers love the chocolate-covered peanut butter candy but, even better, these new M&M's bit into sales of Reese's Peanut Butter Cups.

Mars' surge was due to its various new line extensions. However, the company still needed sales momentum for their basic products.

It looked as though the sleeping giant had at last awakened. More products were pouring out of Mars, although they were extensions of familiar brands. Two chocolate bars were launched in 1992 under the Dove name. They were made of solid milk or dark chocolate and together constituted Mars' first solid chocolate entry in competition with the classic Hershey bars. After the failure of the expensive Sussande bar, this time the company knew to price the Dove Chocolate bar at only 55 cents a bar, below the cost of competing imported European brands. The company also brought out mint and almond M&M's in hopes that their total M&M's revenue might equal as much as $750 million. Of the candy division's jump in income, M&M's Peanut Butter Chocolate Candies claimed about half of the revenue rise.

"It's about time," said a Mars associate of the line extensions. "We have been overly conservative concerning new items over the years."

Hershey was still regarded as the industry's leading innovator but it was not a global company as Mars was. Little had Frank and the elder Forrest Mars known, when they quarreled back in Chicago in the 20s, that Forrest's banishment to England would ensure the future of the Mars business. Or that Forrest's own learning experience would convince him to train his sons in Europe. For Europeans eat greater amounts of sweets than Americans and, although United States consumers had increased their consumption to about 21 pounds by the early 90s, in Europe the average person was annually eating 30 pounds of candy.

Part of the reason behind European's higher candy consumption is that candy is sold in a greater variety of stores in Europe than in the United States. Liquor stores in the United Kingdom, for example, all have candy displays. Additionally, Europeans perceive candy, especially chocolate, as a serious food item whereas Americans see chocolate as an indulgence.

And Mars' greatest advantage over Hershey Foods is its global presence. While Mars had erred in not bringing out new products, Hershey had failed to take advantage of its tremendous international brand recognition after World War II, when Hershey's Milk Chocolate Bar was as well-known in Europe as Coca-Cola. The Hershey's bar was standard GI currency, and the prize of choice for the children of a sugar-starved society under post-war rationing. But Hershey inexplicably ignored overseas markets immediately following the war, and retreated back to the United States. Hershey, in contrast to Mars, has a strong presence outside the United States only in Canada.

"We are a very very very very minor player in Europe," said Ken Wolfe of Hershey. "We have only three small companies and in the market share charts of most companies, we wouldn't even make the chart."

By 1992, only five percent of Hershey's total revenues came from Europe while three-quarters were from the United States. Hershey soon announced, however, that in view of Europeans' brand loyalty, it would expand into Europe through acquisitions of existing companies. In an exploratory move made the year before, Hershey bought the Gubor chocolate business in Germany.

Mars intended not only to hold its share in Europe, but, according to a Mars associate, to enlarge it through "geographic expansion into markets that were previously blocked" which were to include South America, Eastern Europe and the former Soviet Union.

In the United States pet food market, Mars was in third place, behind Ralston Purina and Nestlé. In Europe, though, Mars had been number one since it had introduced that continent to commercial pet food, commanding more than half of Europe's $5 billion market. Because it was selling pet food in more than 30 countries, it restructured its pet food business in 1991 to create a Mars Europet, just as it had restructured its international candy business.

Rice, though Mars' smallest business, stayed the leader among parboiled products with about 25 percent of the American market.

In early 1992, the bad news for Mars was that per capita candy consumption slumped slightly for the first time since 1985, to 20.4 pounds—possibly in response to the nickel increase put in place by Hershey and Mars in 1991. In an attempt to spur sales in this lackluster market, and to retain its lead over Hershey, Mars unwrapped a major consumer refund program that lowered the wholesale price of large packages of M&M's to 1987 levels. For small-size offerings, it offered a "buy one, get one free" coupon. "We feel the category is bogged down and needs a good kick start," said a Mars associate.

Also, the company was offering a nickel back for every pack of candy it sold. Since the wrappers were required to be returned in bundles of 20, with each bundle to be redeemed for $1, the offer was aimed mostly at schools, sports teams, church groups and other large fund raising organizations.

"I expect there will be whole schools eating nothing but the Mars line," said an industry analyst. "This is going to cost Mars beaucoup bucks."

Mars' gambit was obviously intended to push itself farther ahead of Hershey in market share. But Hershey had the last word: two weeks later, it too offered a nickel rebate for each candy bar wrapper. A Hershey spokesperson acknowledged that Hershey's rebate was in direct response to the Mars offer. "Very often, when one manufacturer introduces a promotion, others will counter to stay competitive."

Hershey one-upped Mars by sending coupons for four free candy bars to whomever responded by the end of the first three months of the rebate. Additionally, it showed its considerable philanthropic practices by allowing consumers to have their refunds donated to Children's Miracle Network, which the company has heavily supported since 1987. Since Mars was engaged in no corresponding charitable efforts, it did not make a similar offer to consumers that would have benefited a charity.

Although Nestlé was in a distant third place, Mars felt it needed to distance itself even further by moving into the baking business. It introduced mini-size semi-sweet M&M's, intended for use in cookies, cupcakes and cakes, hoping to make inroads in Nestlé's 59 percent share of the chocolate chip morsel business.

Mars and Hershey were engaged in a fierce contest for leadership in the United States candy industry. By 1991, the two companies accounted for more than 70 percent of candy sales.

## Departures

Although Mars managers had been leaving the company since the early 80s, no absence was felt as deeply as the departure of Al Poe, whose idea it was to alter the American Kal Kan pet food recipe to match the higher-quality European formula. He also was credited for convincing Forrest and John to begin using global brand names, and was responsible for changing the Kal Kan lines to Whiskas and Pedigree.

The globalization of Mars brands continued in its candy division when Poe was promoted to head of marketing. Line extensions were fattened and advertising pumped up. Then, in 1991, Forrest and John restructured its sale division, asking the three candy, pet food and rice sales staffs to coordinate efforts and take over advertising campaigns. This was the most significant organizational change the company had seen in 30 years. Power was taken from marketing and given to the sales division, as they were now directly responsible for making sales goals. Marketing was left with the strategic planning function.

Poe, as head of marketing for the candy division, was initially against these changes. Forrest and John convinced him the switch would be a promotion that might eventually lead to the presidency of the Kal Kan division—the job that Poe had coveted, and that was vacant. At a convention where executives were to address 2,500 sales associates, Poe overheard in a hallway that another executive had just been named president of Kal Kan. The brothers had not even had the courtesy to tell Poe directly that he had lost out on the job.

Poe learned the hard way about the difficulty of working in a family business run by autocrats who cannot loosen control and who will not totally trust anyone who is not a family member. He says that in any decision-making process, when a strong competent manager would challenge Forrest or John, they would revert to the position that they owned the company and their opinions, therefore, outweighed any opposing ideas. It's no wonder that innovative and ambitious executives would inevitably chafe at Mars-imposed restrictions and look for more challenging opportunities elsewhere.

No one was surprised when Poe declined the offer of the Mars brothers to send him to the midwest to head Uncle Ben's rice. Instead, he left the company in December 1991 for a key position at Campbell Soup Co., as president of Vlasic Foods.

In the wake of the void Poe left came the unexpected decision to appoint the head of research and development to head the sales staff. "That's kind of unusual," said a person in the trade. "Normally, you would think they would fill the head sales job with a person with experience in sales."

Others felt that Forrest and John wanted someone in the top sales position with whom they felt comfortable, which narrowed down the field considerably. "The job has a lot less to do with sales than it has to do with market strategy and dealing with John and Forrest," said one man. "It takes a special kind of person."

## Europe '92

Mars was as sensitive to the requirements of the emerging European Community, and its consequences for business, as any other United States corporation. Suddenly, it needed to adapt to an integrated marketplace of 12 countries, each with its own language and culture. Although 1992 was the target date, Mars had taken a leading role more than a decade earlier. One aspect that worried the company was the disclosure rules that were jeopardizing Mars' well-guarded privacy.

The European Commission was emphasizing the need for corporations to be "transparent," which translates into publishing worldwide financial accounts. Any public company is used to this requirement, but for a privately held company, the requirement would be painful. For Forrest and John, letting everyone have access to their company's financial figures would be tantamount to walking down the street naked.

Through its lobbyist, the law firm of Patton Boggs & Blow, bills were introduced in the United States Congress that would prohibit American firms from disclosure of any financial information to foreign governments or the European Commission that was not required to be disclosed by United States law.

Although this bill is just what the Mars company had wanted, the visibility of its introduction interested the media. True to form, Mars withdrew from the arena and denied that the law firm was acting "officially" on its behalf. "I've got a very upset client," said the attorney lobbying for the bill.

Another set of requirements they wanted to overturn was the list of proposed restrictions on European television advertising. The new regulations would have lessened the total number of commercials while making the commercials air in blocks often more than ten minutes long, as was done in West Germany and the Netherlands. Naturally, a number of companies that relied on television ads said the rule would decimate their ability to use television in Europe. In this case, Mars joined H.J. Heinz in its petition to change the ad rules.

In its most important move, Mars began changing its localized brand names to ones that would be global. It made more sense to develop a pan-European brand for the new single European market that consists of 344 million consumers—50 percent more than in the United States. Increasingly, the company has made pan-European marketing its priority.

Because the Mars candy businesses in the United States and in the United Kingdom, for example, had developed separately, the same bar might have been given different names. Marathon Bar, in the United Kingdom, was the same bar as Snickers in the United States. In anticipation of the European Community, in late 1990 the name of the Marathon Bar was changed to Snickers. And the Treets name was dropped in favor of M&M's, and the Raider bar was renamed Twix. Ad campaigns that supported these changes said, "Nothing's changed but the name," and sales rose 25 percent.

Pet foods, too, changed brands with the creation in 1992 of Mars Europet, controlling everything from marketing to accounting for the Mars brands throughout the European Community. Of course, the consolidation of brands within one division made it more difficult for the company to avoid conflicts with a rival brand when choosing advertisers.

Forrest went all out for global branding and even instituted global colors for its products. All Whiskas cat food line labels must be purple, he commanded. The color uniformity confused consumers who were used to different colors on different types of products. Forrest's efforts to build a purple color bloc for Whiskas similar to the well-known red color bloc of Coca-Cola failed.

Not even all global name changes worked. The Treets brand name, thought dead in 1987 as part of Mars' global branding, had to be revived four years later because the M&M's brand that replaced it lost consumers. After all, M&M's had been unknown in the United Kingdom and in Germany until the Treets brand was renamed.

A Mars associate said the name shuffle "may have been a mistake we do not intend to repeat."

But the company actually compromised by renaming the candies M&M's Treets' Selection. The other renamed brands were to remain, as Mars continued to pursue its global branding. Ultimately, the company hoped to use the same names in every country in which the products were sold.

## Lite on Guilt

The dietary hallmark of the 90s is the demonization of fat. People began to scarf down fat-free products regardless of their sugar and sodium content, or their total calorie count. In Candyland, such non-fat sweets as Tootsie Roll Pops, Chuckles and Twizzlers took off—Americans were gaining more weight than ever before, but they felt virtuous as long as they avoided the evil substance. Once again, Mars rode the culture curve.

Just as Mars found that it needed to respond to consumer concerns about nutrition and dental health, it saw soon after its acquisition of DoveBar that people were turning away from high-fat snacks. Almost immediately after Mars bought the company, sales began to lag. Mars poured in marketing dollars to staunch the losses. One way to improve profits, and, at the same time, speak to consumers' desire to cut calories, was to lower the weight of the bar. But when Mars tampered with the traditional 6-ounce size, axing it down by a sizable 37 percent to 3.8 ounces—without reducing the price—customers yelled. (Their ire may also have been aroused by a Consumer Reports article pointing out the reason for the illusory drop in caloric count.) DoveBar sales rose only by one percent and sales of Rondos, its nugget spin-off, fell by seven percent.

Seeing what can happen to a product like DoveBars that's high in fat and calories, Mars quickly moved to protect its stable of candy bars. In 1992, it introduced a line brand extension of its number three-selling bar, Milky Way. This new bar, called Milky Way II, had one-third of its calories squeezed out of it, dropping from the 280 calories of a regular Milky Way to 190 calories.

Mars was the first candy manufacturer to produce a reduced- calorie, reduced-fat candy bar, although sugar-free bars had been produced by other companies. It took six years to manufacture Milky Way II, which has 50 percent fewer fat calories. Calories were cut through, replacing sugar with polydextrose, a complex carbohydrate traditionally used to add body and texture to low-calorie snacks. But the most dramatic difference was made by reducing fat and substituting a low-calorie ingredient called caprenin, made by Procter & Gamble. Caprenin is manufactured from fat molecules found in coconut, palm kernel and rapeseed oils. It has the advantage of not needing approval from the Food and Drug Administration, as would have been required of fat substitutes.

Although light beers had been popular for years, as had diet soft drinks, Mars was the first with the breakthrough light candy bar. The bar was priced at 55 cents, about a dime higher than the regular bar and Milky Way Dark.

The bar was intended to appeal to weight-conscious baby boomers who have cut back on desserts and candy. Industry experts hoped that the low calorie bar would bring back consumers who had been staying away from the high fat and calories of candy bars. But they also warned that if it did not taste very, very good it would fail.

Others thought that once a person made the decision to eat a candy bar, reducing calories by 25 percent would not be a motivator. "If someone is going to go with chocolate, they already have said, 'To heck with the diet,'" said a candy wholesaler. "Personally, I don't see it as being the next soft-drink category."

The director of nutrition at the Center for Science in the Public Interest pointed out that even with a reduced level of fat, the candy bar still retained eight grams, or about 75 calories of fat. But, she added, referring to the sugar and nutritional content, "even if they took out all the fat, this candy bar would not turn into a cantaloupe."

Of course, all eyes turned on Hershey Foods. "We're behind, but we hope to have a low-fat bar soon," said its chief financial officer.

Analysts wondered if the reduced calorie Milky Way II would be able to close the gap between it and Hershey, by now at a narrow three percent. "This could make the difference," speculated a candy industry executive.

By September, 1992 Hershey Foods was test-marketing a new reduced-fat, reduced-calorie bar in two midwestern markets. The company had not named the bar, which, unlike Mars' Milky Way II, was not a spin-off bar. A Hershey spokesperson said, "While Hershey's Reduced Calorie and Fat candy bar was not designed to taste exactly like a Hershey's Milk Chocolate Bar, we believe consumers who are looking for a lower calorie and fat candy bar will find it to be an excellent product." Both bars used caprenin.

Over time, these two low-fat bars have made a poor showing. Hershey dropped its bar. Mars, still hopeful that its bar will catch on, has renamed it Milky Way Lite and is keeping it on life support.

## Behind Bars

Mars suddenly found itself in trouble from an unexpected quarter. Though it's not known whose brainchild the disastrous 1991 ad campaign was, it's a fair bet that Jackie was not part of the company's decision-making process. The offending ad, for Twix cookie bar, poked fun at all-girls schools. The television spot showed a mother threatening to send her daughter to a girls' school; next, the girl is seen staring out from what looks like the bars of a prison. Although the linkage between these images and eating Twix bars was hazy to some viewers, they did get the message that attending a girls' school was comparable to going to prison.

Within a few days, two organizations representing more than 70 independent girls' schools—including the high school from which Jackie had graduated—protested the advertisement. In an assertive letter, the Coalition of Girls' Schools and the Coalition of Girls' Boarding Schools demanded that the ads be dropped. "The ad perpetuates a misconception about girls' schools that is held only by those who have never visited a girls' school."

Using muscle that Mars could understand, some of the member schools yanked Mars products from their campus vending machines. They also had students draft letters that threatened a boy(girl?)cott of Mars candy.

Mars responded by trying to cast itself as David to the school association's as Goliath. Noting that the association had hired a public relations firm, a Mars associate plaintively said, "It is unfortunate that the coalition did not see fit to contact somebody in the company before utilizing the resources of a public relations counselor. The commercial was originally intended to be [humorous] but has turned out to be disturbing to some people, and for this we apologize."

And in a rare corporate release of information about the Mars family, the company disclosed that all of Forrest Jr.'s, John's and Jackie's daughters had graduated from private girls' schools.

Predictably, Mars' reaction was defensive . . . and offensive: in a prime example of throwing stones while living in a glass house, the company sniffed that the schools took themselves too seriously, and didn't appreciate the joke. In turn, the coalition spokesperson rebuked Mars for its implication that its members had lost their sense of humor. "This is sort of like librarian jokes, which are probably funny unless you're a librarian," she said. "Stereotypical jokes are fun unless you're the brunt of them."

## The Green Ones

The Mars company's own inability to see humor when the tables were turned against it was evident in 1992 when it quashed the sale of The Green Ones, produced by a company that had sprung up as a gambit to take advantage of the popularity of green M&M's. Over the years, the putative power of green M&M's as aphrodisiacs had taken on mythological proportions among young people and particularly, among Californians. As one University of Colorado freshman said, "I think it's a psychological thing. The more you believe, the better your chances of getting lucky."

In fact, would-be Romeos who wrote Mars asking about the power of green M&M's would get a very serious response: "Although many consumers ask us about the special qualities of green M&M's chocolate candies, we cannot explain any extraordinary 'powers' attributed to this color, either scientifically or medically."

One young attorney, considering a business venture, decided to see how far she could push the rumor. "I thought this one was the most fun," Wendy Jaffe said. She quit her $70,000 a year job and founded Cool Chocolates, Inc. with $20,000 she raised with her own money and with cash from her father, also a lawyer, and her mother, a teacher. Jaffe began manufacturing an M&M's-like candy that was produced only in green. She called her product The Green Ones, after she had registered the name as a trademark in March 1992. She made sure her packaging did not resemble M&M's—after all, she is a lawyer—although she did include figure drawings that somewhat resembled the cartoonish character that M&M's has used in its advertising campaigns. The power of the green myth was so strong that Jaffe quickly licensed rights to Hallmark for use in greeting cards.

Unlike Mars, Jaffe openly linked her product to the hope of romance. The Green Ones carried a warning label that read: IN CASE OF OVERINDULGENCE take a cold shower or hit yourself over the head with a frying pan."

The red lipstick-kiss-covered packaging also includes testimonials from such pleased customers as a man in Lackawanna, Pennsylvania, who said, "Ever since The Green One came to town, barely anyone goes bowling anymore," and from Saul Rabinowitz, age 93, who said, "I didn't know I had it in me."

In October, Mars filed suit in federal court charging trademark infringement and unfair competition. It claimed to be the only manufacturer of aphrodisiac-rumored candy. The company stated that Cool Chocolates "is marketing the product as 'the only candy with a reputation' when, in fact, it is only Mars' product which has a reputation of special powers in the public's mind."

Jaffe was disgusted. "The irony is that they've tried for years to distance themselves from the myth."

An M&M's spokesman responded, "We simply want to make sure the consumer isn't confused." M&M's did not object to the rumor, the spokesman said (as if the company could do anything about it!), but he compared the notoriety to the mythic "alligators living in New York City sewers."

After Mars sued, Jaffe received tremendous publicity. Not only did the newspapers seize upon her story, but she was featured in *People* magazine and—in an obvious association with her product's power—she was a contestant on the raunchy television show "Studs."

The court, however, ruled that Jaffe had to change her packaging and the name of her product, which she renamed Greenies after Mars refused her offer to put a disclaimer on the packaging that would have dissociated her candy from M&M's.

"They want to put me out of business," Jaffe claimed. "But this legend was created by the public," she said in retrospect.

## Townies vs. Mars

But now the brothers stepped into a hornet's nest outside the boundaries of Candyland per se. Mars, Inc., as any major company does, has picked up considerable real estate holdings over the years. One of the Mars family trusts, for example, owns land in Phoenix, Arizona on which sits a 47-acre office-shopping- hotel retail development called Colonnade.

In 1992, the company began to plan what turned out to be a controversial development in Montgomery County, Maryland, across the Potomac River from Mars' McLean headquarters. C-G Realty, a subsidiary of Mars, Inc., owned 843 acres of land upcounty in an agricultural zone near Laytonsville, Maryland. The acreage had been bought in the 70s by Forrest Sr. Later, the company had considered the land for a corporate retreat and had even sent Jack Nicklaus to Laytonsville to check the acreage out for a golf course.

C-G Realty—whose president is Vito Spitaleri, Mars' corporate treasurer—also owned another 300 acres north of the same town. When the property was bought, zoning laws stipulated a two-acre minimum, says a local developer. In the following years Montgomery County down-zoned the land to 25 acres, which diminished its value, unknown to Mars; the company had been so preoccupied by other concerns that it had not been following zoning actions as closely as it should have.

The Mars subsidiary joined several adjacent landowners to propose a project called Rolling Ridge, named after the farm of one of the other landowners. Rolling Ridge was projected as having perhaps as many as 720 houses, with 2,500 residents. The houses would be valued at about $500,000. Thirty acres of land were proposed to be rezoned for commercial development.

Some local residents feared that the area's population would increase tenfold and that Montgomery County would have to shoulder a multi-million-dollar burden for a development of this size in an agricultural reserve without public facilities. Laytonsville, after all, is a country town with a handful of antiques stores, and where many residents are still dependent upon well-water.

The town of Laytonsville was divided between those who were optimistic that the project would bring jobs and those who distrusted the idea of change and the promises of town improvements. One reason the townspeople were skeptical was that Rolling Ridge was associated with Mars, Inc., which is well known in the Washington area as a secretive company. Citizens feared the worst of Mars, and although Mayor Charles White had met once with Vito Spitaleri and was behind a proposed referendum to give voters the chance to vote directly on annexing the land to Laytonsville, the proposal never got that far. Making the 245 Laytonsville voters especially nervous was Mars' retaining an area public relations firm, Geigerich & Associates, to serve as its liaison.

Although the way in which the company distanced itself from the project was typical of Mars, its attitude angered Laytonsville residents, who were more accustomed to driving their kids to 4-H meetings than to dealing with a public relations firm. Ultimately, the scheme folded. The land Mars owns is still used for agricultural purposes and the company still hopes to return the property to its original value.

## An Unhappy Marriage

The Rolling Ridge debacle was not the only real estate dispute in which the Mars family got embroiled. Jackie's marriage to Hank was a disappointment to both of them, but one of the few activities that they had mutually enjoyed was improving Hickory Corner. Hank came to appreciate Jackie's eye for landscaping. And she upgraded the property in 1991 by spending nearly as much money for the new wing with extra bedrooms for her children's visits, the riding ring, the kennel and the refashioned stable as she had on the original purchase of the estate. Jackie in turn recognized Hank's exquisite taste in antique furnishings and valued the many fine pieces he had brought to Hickory Corners from his own collection.

But renovation and refurbishment of property was not enough to keep the relationship in good shape. Hank, ever the optimist, recognized their differences and tried to work them out by doing as much as he could to keep Jackie happy. Her favorite activity is riding. Though Hank himself is an outdoorsman, and his business is riding boots, he was never much interested in equestrian sports, preferring to shoot quail with his English setters, or play golf or tennis. Horses were his work, not his life.

But Jackie, it sometime seemed, was only happy on horseback. So in order to keep her company and share her favorite sport, Hank made an effort to enjoy riding. He had hoped to have fun. But every time he got on horseback, Jackie would criticize him. He was doing this wrong and he was doing that wrong. "Why can't you ride as well as I do?" Jackie would complain. It was not long before Hank became totally discouraged and refused to ride.

Hank also had to put up with Jackie's temper storms, which he described as sometimes violent. "If I said anything, she blew up. Jackie's got her father's temper and when she loses it, it's not a pretty sight."

One fall evening in 1989, shortly after the year's *Forbes* 400 list had included Jackie's name as one of the wealthiest 400 people or families in the United States, the couple was invited to a dinner party at a nearby estate. Of course, the Bedminster area where Jackie and Hank lived also was home to Malcolm Forbes' showplace country home. The hostess had invited Forbes to her party and, as a special courtesy, seated the colorful publisher at the same table as Jackie and Hank. Hank was thrilled at the opportunity to spend an evening chatting with a fascinating celebrity like Forbes.

But Jackie was enraged when she saw the seating arrangement. She had been furious that *Forbes* magazine had violated her privacy by printing her name in its "rich list" and she irrationally blamed Malcolm Forbes—personally—for her inclusion. She stormed up to the hostess and threatened, "I will not sit next to that man." She said she would walk out if the seating arrangement were not changed. So Hank never got to talk with Malcolm Forbes.

As Jackie's involvement in corporate work increased, she suggested that the couple move to Middleburg, the horsey enclave near her father's Marland estate. Hank resisted, as he still had his business in Manhattan and felt that the hunt country of Virginia might be too pastoral for his taste.

Their marital woes were put aside briefly when Hank learned he had colon cancer in 1991. Naturally, he was frightened and appreciated Jackie's support and kindness when he first entered the hospital. But while he was at Hickory Corner recovering, Jackie left him alone to travel for Mars and to fox hunt in Middleburg.

Although their marriage was deteriorating, Jackie continued to support the household lavishly. She paid all expenses, including the salaries of one full-time and one part-time secretary, a housekeeper, a maid, a laundress, a farm manager, four full-time stable and horse workers, and a gardener.

That year, also, Jackie had gifted Hank with a stock portfolio valued at $74,000. The following June, when Hank decided to sell his share of the E. Vogel boot company to his son and settle real estate upon his daughter, she paid off the mortgage on Hank's Vermont property. Jackie had already given gifts to his children and grandchild totaling more than $180,000.

However, she was careful to keep her assets from co-mingling with his. Ever since their marriage, she had always refused to list Hank on her credit accounts. Never had Jackie opened a line of credit on which her husband appeared as an authorized signatory. Every time they went out to dinner, she slipped him her credit card so it would appear as if he were paying. Nor did they share a joint account checking account: all of the couple's respective assets and incomes were maintained separately.

## Jackie Files for Divorce

The next year, Hank became ill again and was diagnosed with cancer of the prostate. His treatment was fully successful, but he felt abandoned as he lay in the hospital. He felt especially wounded when he heard that Jackie hoped this second illness would eliminate him from her life. He knew the marriage was not going great, but at least it was going—he had thought.

When his doctors discharged him from the hospital, Jackie sent a car and driver to pick him up, rather than come herself. She remained in the house only a day or two after he returned home before leaving to travel for the Mars company. Hank was very upset at what he perceived as his welfare playing second fiddle to the family business.

The last cancer scare had spurred Hank's realization that life was uncertain and should be lived meaningfully. Marriage to a woman who was rarely in residence, and who avoided being alone with her husband when she did see him, was not what Hank wanted. Jackie had also stopped having sexual relations with Hank, and he saw that as symptomatic of the marriage's problems. He began to rankle at Jackie's treatment of him, feeling she was cheating him of the years that he had left. He was also slowly realizing that, when they had courted, Jackie had painted a false picture of their future together.

Worse still, the couple's arguments escalated. Jackie's anger was expressed by throwing objects and slapping, reports Hank. One time, Hank was upstairs in the master bedroom wing on his exercise bicycle when his wife unexpectedly came home to find that he had moved some of his clothes into an upstairs closet that she considered hers, although it had been mostly empty. When Jackie saw Hank's clothes, she screamed in anger and began throwing the garments on the floor. Hank kept riding the bike, watching her. Enraged and frustrated because she was unable to extract a reaction from her husband, who was doing his best to ignore the tantrum, Jackie pulled the louvered closet door out of its hinge, leaving it half-hanging.

On other occasions when Jackie was riled, Hank says, she threw a cup of coffee at him, hit him in the face with a hair brush and threw stones at his car. Once, the couple began arguing in the car as Hank was driving and Jackie, losing her temper, struck him.

Although Jackie disliked talking about (as opposed to venting) her feelings, the word "divorce" did begin coming up in conversation. Once, when she threatened to remove his belongings from the Bedminster house and to bar him access, Hank consulted an attorney because he was fearful of losing his home and wanted to learn what his rights were.

Hank had been in counseling at an earlier stage in his life. He found he had learned a great deal about himself then and thought therapy could be very helpful now. But when he suggested to Jackie on several occasions that they see a marriage counselor together, she categorically refused and escalated his proposals into arguments.

Late in 1992, Jackie announced to Hank that she had purchased three houses in Virginia, unbeknownst to him. She suggested that Hank continue to live in New Jersey while she would live in the estate she was planning in the area of The Plains, Virginia, just several miles from the Marland estate where she had grown up. Her idea was that they would see each other occasionally and travel together, but live apart. With this proposition, Hank saw where his marriage was headed.

Living apart was what Jackie's parents had done and she saw nothing wrong with repeating this pattern. For his part, Hank said, he had always felt that her parents' marriage was "strange and inappropriate and was certainly unsatisfactory to me and not what I expected of a marriage." He was disgusted at Jackie's proposition and wanted to have nothing to do with the type of false relationship that the senior

Marses had lived. When he refused to agree to her proposal, Jackie filed for divorce on January 22, 1993.

Jackie now felt that home was her estate in The Plains, which she called Stonehall Farm. During the work week, she frequently stayed at Audrey's Watergate apartment, now in Forrest Sr.'s name, so that she only had a 15-minute commute across the Potomac River to the company's headquarters.

Jackie took care to renovate the formal apartment, with its Louis Quatorze reproduction furniture, so that her elderly father, who had been handicapped by several strokes, could visit. Doorways were widened and bathroom fixtures were made accessible. "Jackie would do anything to make her dad happy," said a woman who had known the family for many years.

Jackie enjoyed the Watergate apartment and its view of the next door Saudi Embassy and the John F. Kennedy Center for Performing Arts. Robert Strauss, the Democratic party powerbroker, was her next-door neighbor. The garden was not as beautiful as when Audrey was living and the dark brown paint the family chose did little to enhance the architecture. Then again, the entire apartment was a little odd, thought visitors who had to walk under a spiral staircase in order to get to the roof deck. Nor did one guest appreciate a characteristic touch of Jackie's in the powder room—a lucite toilet seat embedded with gold coins. "One step above a trailer park," he sniffed.

Jackie continued to be cautious about her personal security, even in this well-managed building where she lived—and still lives on weekdays—with a full-time maid. In fact, she was not content until she had deadbolt locks installed in every door so that once she was locked in for the night, no one else could enter the apartment.

Jackie's anger at Hank seemed to increase after she petitioned for a divorce. She threatened to throw him out of "her house," as she called Hickory Corner it, and sent her attorney to lecture the household staff about not performing duties for Hank. In addition, the attorney told the staff not to communicate with Hank. If they could not follow the new rules, he said, they could "feel free to leave."

The staff was required to split their work so as to avoid assisting Hank in any way. For example, the dog groomer now groomed only Jackie's dogs and bypassed Hank's. The newspaper was canceled, along with magazine subscriptions, and the liquor cabinet was locked.

One weekend in March, Jackie removed all the food from the Hickory Corner refrigerator and locked her office so that Hank could not enter. Later, despite an understanding between the attorneys that Jackie's furniture would not yet be removed from Hickory Corner, Hank returned home after being out-of-town to find Jackie had entered with furniture movers and taken out belongings.

In what seemed to Hank to be an overt act of harassment, Jackie hired a security guard who would follow Hank from room to room, who played her radio at a high volume and who appeared obtrusively in the room when Hank had visitors and refused to leave. Since the couple had not hired security for the house before, and since the guard was present while Jackie was in Middleburg, it appeared that the guard's purpose was to interfere with whatever enjoyment Hank was getting out of remaining in Hickory Corner.

At Christmas Jackie told the Hickory Corner staff, whom she rarely saw at this point, that it had been a bad year for her financially and that they should not expect their usual Christmas bonus. She finally came through with their money but her pose of being hard-up was a little hard for most people to take.

# Seven

# The Chocolate Wars

Jackie's personal problems paralleled the trauma felt within the company when, in 1992, Hershey nosed Mars out of its short-lived lead. Hershey was able to finish the year with 34.9 percent of the market, compared to Mars' 29.9 percent, causing a Mars associate to state defensively that market share was not the only measure of success for the company.

The best news for Hershey was that sales of its candy bars had jumped 18.7 percent by the beginning of 1993, while sales of Mars candy bars improved by only a sluggish 1.4 percent. Mars' poor showing was in contradiction to an industry-wide sales increase attributed to its ability to hold down prices, due to the 50 percent drop in cocoa that occurred between 1986 and 1992.

Mars was further disappointed by its sales of Milky Way II, which was not carving a new path for light candy bars. It was felt that Milky Way Dark and the new M&M's line extensions were hurting sales of Milky Way bar's and M&M's candies' core brands. The company began plans to re-market Milky Way II as Milky Way Lite.

In 1993, Hershey widened its lead over Mars in the United States, foreshadowing a trend that would continue through 1995. Respective market shares were 27 percent for Hershey and 23.4 percent for Mars. Hershey's weapons were its new products, brought to the public's attention through increased advertising, which the company raised by 17 percent. It was growing at three times the rate of the confectionery industry overall.

"Hershey had a mission and accomplished it," said one industry specialist. Additionally, its bagged and seasonal candy that accounts for a rising percentage of sales had proven more popular than Mars candies. Seasonal candy has been a growing market in the 90s, leaping up by 20 percent in just one year. The biggest shift has benefited Easter candy, which is now the largest of holiday candy categories with sales of about $500 million. Until the early 90s, the industry had left Easter to a few specialty manufacturers. Realizing the potential of that holiday, by the mid-90s the major companies were busy putting a pastel shade on their wrapping or manufacturing special egg-shaped treats.

Halloween is next most popular candy holiday and is growing, with candy manufacturers seeing these sales pushing over $1 billion by the mid-90s. Christmas follows. (Since the popularity of boxed chocolates has fallen off, Valentine's Day is the least popular of the four holidays with the candy-buying public.)

A decade earlier, candy manufacturers had perceived Halloween as of increasing importance to potential sales. As a result, the three major industry associations—the Chocolate Manufacturers Association, the National Candy Brokers Association and the National Confectioners Association—attempted to pressure Congress to extend Daylight Savings Time through the first Sunday of November. Their reasoning was the extra daylight hour would presumably encourage more parents to allow their children to trick-or-treat for an additional hour, which would translate into greater candy sales. "This is the first time ever that business has taken a look at this and realized that it means dollars in their pockets," said a lobbyist. But the bill that was introduced in the House went nowhere, and the candy industry is no longer pushing for an extension of Daylight Savings Time.

As Mars fell further behind Hershey, it looked as if what was hurting it were its many line extensions. Apparently, customers became confused at the number of spin-offs. Mars had hoped that those customers who bought, for example, Peanut Butter Snickers would do so rather than choosing, say, Hershey's Reese's Peanut Butter Cup. Instead, it looked as if the customers were choosing Peanut Butter Snickers over regular Snickers. The Mars line extensions were eating into their own core brands.

In fact, as *The Wall Street Journal* noted, even their core brands, like Milky Way, 3 Musketeers and Snickers, "are all fairly similar."

Also inadequate was the way that Mars was relying on one flavor as the magic ingredient to transform their traditional products. The monotonous consistency of three peanut butter line extensions—M&M's Peanut Butter, Peanut Butter Snickers and PB Max—may have been too thick for consumers to swallow. At the same time, Mars also recalled the Bounty coconut bar it had brought from England, plus two Twix line extensions.

Partly to blame for the blinkered vision was the continuing top-staff turnover at Mars. Internal policy changes took their toll: a new retirement program intended to reduce the bloat of six-figure incomes meant losses of up to 300 senior marketing and sales staff. Vendors felt the pinch of tighter credit practices, while retailers and wholesalers were angered by the company's abrupt halt in promotions, with no attempt to work with the middlemen to compensate for the lack of special discounts. Hershey, while also cutting down on promotional money, had shown more flexibility and concern for the needs of distributors and retailers.

Most devastating to Mars was the edging out of the traditional number one brand, Snickers, by Reese's Peanut Butter Cups. Despite Mars' having outspent Hershey in advertising, Reese's came in at 5.2 percent of the candy market in 1993 compared to five percent for Snickers.

Mars refused to acknowledge the defeat. "By all the statistics we have, Snickers is the best-selling candy bar," insisted an associate.

## Hershey Hugs the Lead

Hershey's romance with the public further flowered in its August 1993 introduction of Hershey's Hugs, a white-and-milk chocolate version of its Hershey's Kisses. Hugs was its second line extension of Kisses; the first was Hershey's Kisses With Almonds, brought out in 1990. The new product was an integral part of its strategy to maintain the lead over Mars. And the company expected sales of Hugs to cannibalize Kisses' sales by less than three percent.

Hershey had been working on the white-and-brown-striped "kiss"-shaped candy for more than 15 years; its path was smoothed by the manufacturing innovations it had devised for the chocolate Kiss with an almond inside. The new process for the almond Kiss, which involves using a mold, could be adapted so that a miniature chocolate Kiss could go inside, with a white-striped chocolate Hug on the outside. A team with members representing different departments formed to manufacture and launch the product in top speed, less than 18 months from its test marketing.

"When you introduce a new product, it's not something that someone in a lab develops, and someone else figures out marketing and someone else goes and sells," says Hershey's leader Ken Wolfe. "It's a collective effort, everyone working closely in a team effort. You can have a fabulous product and have a great marketing concept but you ultimately have to execute in order for that new product to be a success."

One of the most striking components of this introduction is that Hershey took the care to do it right: rather than just introducing a white-chocolate Kiss, which would have been simply another Kiss line extension, it took on the challenge of finding a more exciting way to combine white chocolate with traditional chocolate. This innovation took advantage of the new perception of white chocolate (flavored cocoa butter, with the brown-colored liquor extracted) as a gourmet treat, while providing a visual and gustatory novelty in the striped effect. Hershey's trailblazing was in sharp contrast to the timid Mars strategy of making a new product by merely adding peanut butter to basic brands.

With Hugs, Hershey was appealing both to young people and to baby boomers, who show a preference for bite-size products and who relish white chocolate. Hershey also introduced the Cookies 'n' Mint chocolate bar and Hershey's Special Dark chocolate bar, and reformulated Bar None. Additionally, it brought out such interesting non-chocolate candies as Amazin' Fruit, aimed at young children and owned the Twizzlers candy brand. Hershey, however, had to pull its Hershey's Reduced Calorie & Fat from its test marketing regions the year before due to lack of consumer interest.

At midyear, Hershey was maintaining its position—and its gain was Mars' loss. Still being criticized were Mars' various line extensions. *Advertising Age* noted that "analysts believe M&M/Mars has faltered by putting too much emphasis on line extensions at the expense of core brands," whereas "Hershey thought out its new product launches—they were new items, new categories, new flavorings. A lot of the Mars products didn't meet these needs." And its upheaval in marketing staff was noted.

In 1994, it was obvious even at Mars that its line-extension strategy was not working. Although Snickers sales went up one percent, Snickers Peanut Butter went down two percent. M&M's Plain lost five percentage points, while its extension M&M's Peanut Butter went down nine percent in sales, and M&M's Almonds dropped a whopping 22 percent. Twix Cookie bars were down 12 percent, while their extensions plunged: Twix Peanut Butter was down 75 percent from the previous year and Twix Cookie 'N' Cream plummeted by 81 percent.

It looked as if the path to success followed new products, not line extensions. "The products that Hershey comes out with are much more innovative and new than the Mars products," said an analyst. Hershey's Cookies 'n' Mint bar was a different taste from Hershey's Milk Chocolate bar and it captured consumers' imaginations. Hershey's Hugs was turning out to be a phenomenal success, and was not hurting sales of Hershey's Kisses in any meaningful way. The company also planned a thick candy bar called Nuggets to be introduced in 1995.

"Hershey looks at a line extension as a new product and market it as such," said the analyst. "Mars treats a line extension as a line extension."

Another analyst in the industry summed it up: "Almost everything M&M/Mars has done has been a failure."

At the end of March 1994 Mars was showing 26.1 percent of the market share while Hershey was a full eight percentage points higher at 34.1 percent.

Mars seemed to take a cue from its dipping sales and was starting to retrench from the assault of line extensions that began in 1989. It planned to drop its single-serving flavored Twix bars, limiting sales of the Peanut Butter, Cookie 'N'

Creme, and Fudge 'N' Crunchy flavors to packaging as part of a multipack. Only the core Twix caramel bar would be sold separately.

Still, by April 1994 the core Mars brands had dropped 20 percent from the preceding 12-month period. M&M's were down a full 12 percent. It almost seemed as if headquarters was concentrating on expansion in China and Russia rather than picking up dropped percentage points in the United States.

In fact, Mars abroad was fighting another family-owned candy company, an Italian company named Ferrero. The site of the battle was in Germany, where Ferrero had established special candy bars that appealed to young children under the Kinder chocolate line. Mars had been Germany's largest confectioner, but just as Hershey had passed up the company in the 80s in the United States, so had Ferrero outstripped Mars in Germany that same decade. Mars was now pushing back in Germany with a children's line under the Milky Way brand umbrella that emphasized the brand's high milk content to stress nutrition. The company had been trying to introduce this children's line since 1987 but had not been able to pull it together until 1994. Nevertheless, the smart money in Germany is on Ferrero, as it is considered a more innovative company.

At the same time, the British press was reporting a loss for the Mars U.K. holding company, Food Manufacturers. The company, Forrest Sr.'s flagship, was reported to have actually lost more than 1.4 million British pounds the year before. This was incredibly bad news to a company that had prided itself on a strong presence in England. Moreover, the British market was of immense importance to Mars because the British eat more Mars products each year than any other nation, including the United States.

Similarly, in 1992 the company had lost money in Britain on its Whiskas brand cat food. In the United States, Whiskas has lost half its market share since its global branding strategy. And again, the company launched Expert, an upscale health food for dogs. However, consumers who are interested in buying this type of fancy pooch grub tend to purchase it from their veterinarian or from the new pet markets—not at the grocery store, where Mars was trying to push Expert.

Mars was facing heavy competition in Europe from nearly everyone, in 1992 placing second in market share, behind Nestlé SA. Even Hershey, in an attempt to be a player, bought Sperlari and Overspecht, the Italian and German companies. Hershey also increased sales in Asia, especially in Singapore, Malaysia and Korea. Elsewhere in Europe, Philip Morris bought both Jacobs Suchard and Freia Marabou, adding a total of nearly $5 billion in sales to its bottom line for about 15 percent of market share, following close on Mars' heels. Cadbury Schweppes bought a number of small companies, plus the larger French business, Chocolat Poulain.

Mars also fought Ferrero in the United States, where the Italian company was selling a popular chocolate spread called Nutella that had been the spread leader for several years. Mars fought back with a Milky Way Chocolate & Hazelnut Spread, and by doing so, tried to jump on the spread bandwagon to expand into this new snack that had proven popular in Europe. Hershey, of course, had already made solid inroads with its Reese's peanut butter spread, ranking fifth in the category that Mars had just entered.

In ice cream novelty bars, Mars was third: behind Unilever, with 20 percent of the market in the United States and Nestlé, with 16.5 percent. Mars fell behind with 7 percent; Eskimo Pie, a Richmond, Virginia company, followed on its heels with 6.5 percent.

Hershey Foods seemed to be ascending in this market as it teamed with the Good Humor-Breyers company to produce a new ice cream novelty called Reese's Peanut Butter Ice Cream Cups, to be introduced in 1995. The company's goal was to take advantage of the very popular Reese's candy bar and use its flavors in an ice cream product. Hershey chose Good Humor as its link because it "has the expertise and distribution outlets in ice cream that we don't have," said a spokesperson for Hershey. "We have a good product name and presence. It's a nice match." And one guaranteed to make Mars watchful.

There were more stomachaches on the international front, this time with the Uncle Ben's rice brand. In early 1993, the company introduced its Uncle Ben's to South Africa. But stymied by brand loyalty and retail problems, its estimate of a three- to five-percent share of the rice market within a year proved illusory, and the company made no serious inroads. Mars mounted its usual window dressing of being in it for the long haul as it wrapped its advertisements around a chauvinistic display, featuring a box of Uncle Ben's rice—sporting an updated, more genteel-looking black chef—nestled in the American flag.

One advertisement that ended up being cut back was the spring 1994 Starburst low-fat frozen yogurt ad; it carried the fortuitously inflammatory tagline "Turn Loose the Juice." Although O.J. Simpson had never been part of the advertising campaign, the company feared that consumers might assume the slogan referred to the controversial jailed celebrity. Mars laconically called the coincidence "unfortunate."

The company had already shown that it could be sensitive to image problems. Five years earlier, a television industry newsletter called *Market Shares* discovered that Mars, with the help of its ad agencies, had compiled a list of television shows—dubbed the hit list—on which it refused to air its ads. Among the more than 50 shows that Mars disapproved of were the popular *Miami Vice, Sally Jessy Raphael, 20-20* and *Golden Girls.* Several other companies were reported to keep hit lists, including Pizza Hut and Exxon, although no business targeted as many prohibited television shows as Mars.

"We have a policy which states that we wish to associate our advertising with shows that reflect the corporation's principles and its responsibilities as a good corporate citizen," said a Mars spokesperson.

The company was miffed when Nestlé, which had heard that President Bill Clinton's favorite candy bar is their own Baby Ruth, ran an ad boasting: "When the new President said his favorite candy bar is Baby Ruth, nobody Snickered." Certainly no one at Mars even cracked a smile at the ad, but they filed suit seeking an injunction against Nestlé's running the advertisement again.

The year ended on a small note of cheer for Mars, however. A news story flashed across the globe that three British climbers marooned in the Caucasus Mountains were able to stay alive for six days by eating the three Mars bars they had stashed in their pockets.

This tale promoted a healthier image of Mars bars than the rumor that had been spreading for nearly 30 years. In 1967, the arrest of Mick Jagger and Keith Richards of the Rolling Stones rock group, along with singer Marianne Faithfull and others for drug possession, flashed a false story about a Mars bar around the world. The West Sussex constabulary raid found not only drugs but a group of stoned musicians and a Marianne Faithfull, naked except for a fur rug that she had pulled over herself. Although the truth was that Faithfull had just emerged from the bath and had grabbed the rug for cover, the police jumped to more lurid conclusions.

Soon a rumor was circulating, related by Faithfull in her autobiography. Shortly after their trial, Jagger said to Faithfull, "You know what they're saying about us in Wormwood Scrubs, they're saying that when the cops arrived they caught me eatin' a Mars Bar out of your pussy."

Faithfull continues, "I laughed it off, but my amusement began to wane when the damn story established itself as a set piece of British folklore. Mick retrieving a Mars Bar from my vagina, indeed!"

## Men From Mars Invade Russia!

Less than a week after the New Year, 1991, Mars Inc. put their first group of candy bars on sale . . . for rubles. Twenty-three tons of Snickers, Milky Way, Mars and Raider (Twix) candy bars were exported to Russia for purchase. The company announced that the candy bars would be on sale for one day only, commencing at 9:00 a.m. By dawn, hundreds of Muscovites were queued along Kalinin Prospekt, stoically trying to ignore the near-zero temperature and steady snowfall. Despite a two-hour wait, at noon there remained a line of 400 sweet-toothed Russians.

The nation was in the middle of a sugar shortage and had been craving hard-to-come-by candy. When the political structure of the Soviet Union collapsed, state subsidies to confectioners ended. These manufacturers had no currency to buy sugar and cocoa, so factories sat idle. By 1992, Russia had no candy that was made within the country. Candy was on sale inside special stores for foreigners, but only in exchange for foreign currency. So the Mars candy was deeply appreciated, even at $2.80—or a third of a day's pay—for four bars, one of each kind.

A few months later, M&M's were exported for sale to the USSR and the first Mars ad campaign in the Soviet Union broke. Mars began plans to expand into several former Eastern bloc countries, including Hungary, Romania, Bulgaria, Croatia, Slovenia, Bosnia and Albania. M&M's, once introduced, were not as popular as Snickers because the Russians prefer a more filling candy. In fact, the radio and television ad slogan boasts of Snicker bar's "fat, fat layer of chocolate."

Mars' slogan, *Delo ili Igra, Sneekerz* translates to "Work or Play, Snickers," which was reminiscent of the decade-old Snickers slogan in the United Kingdom, "Mars makes you active for work, sport and games." (In a satire on this familiar European tagline, a German condom maker packaged its condoms with a Mars logo and the words, "Mars makes you active for sex, sports and games," until Mars stopped the company from distributing the "Mars" condoms.)

By moving into Russia as soon as it had, Mars locked up the chocolate market there by the middle of 1993. Even officials at the company were surprised at how readily Russians took to the candy, especially to the Snickers bar. Mars was boosted by Central Europe Trust, an 80-person firm focused on moving blue-chip businesses into Eastern Europe.

Mars not only moved quickly, but reacted more flexibly than other western companies that, for example, sold its goods for hard currency rather than rubles. "Mars had done its homework," acknowledged a distributor. "Anyone can be successful here like Mars, if they have quality products and spend about $100,000 in the first three months on advertising." By 1993, the cost of a Snickers bar had been scaled back to about 35 cents, making it an affordable candy bar. Mars was careful to keep its candy bar cost stable as Russia's currency devalued; other Western companies had raised their ruble prices but Mars felt that their long-range purpose would be better served by keeping prices as level as possible.

Monthly sales were estimated at between $10 and $20 million, which was an excellent start—and, more significantly, it was the foundation for a future in Russia. Hershey products, in contrast, were totally unknown in Russia and other former Soviet bloc countries; and while Nestlé was doing business in Russia, it was selling only non-candy products there. By moving fast and aggressively, Mars captured a new market for itself.

By the time Russian candy companies were able to begin manufacturing after the political turmoil ended, Mars was already in place with its products. One of Russia's best-known chocolate companies, one that carries the patriotic name Red October, tried to raise equity in a privatization effort during Russia's transition to a market economy. Bankers were having a difficult time finding clients to buy shares. "Russians mainly seem to be eating Mars bars and Snickers," remarked one banker.

## Viskas

One barrier facing Mars candy was the high tariff Russia imposed in 1993—up to 35 percent. Since Russians were eating Snickers bars exported from Waco, Texas, that state's United States senator became active when she arrived in Moscow. Although Senator Kay Bailey Hutchinson came as part of a seven-member Senate Armed Services Committee delegation—in Moscow to discuss military issues—she was able to have the panel's chairman, Senator Sam Nunn of Georgia, steer the conversation to the subject of high Russian taxes.

Hutchinson first mentioned oil industry tariffs, then turned to the topic of Snickers. She had been clued in to its tariff problems at a Senate prayer breakfast by industry lobbyist Mark Andrews. "He said, 'By the way, since you are going to Russia, you should know that they are raising the tariffs on Snickers, which is the most popular candy bar in Russia. The executives at Mars are very concerned about it, since they have been doing very well in Russia,'" remembers Hutchinson.

"I said 'Fine,' I'd bring it up."

Andrews also told Hutchinson that Russia represented a $300 million annual market for Snickers, and that sales decreased once the tariff was put in place.

The next step for Mars was to build manufacturing plants in Russia so that Mars products—now including novelty ice cream bars—would not have to be imported. In 1993 the company's subsidiary, Master Foods Russia, received permission to build three factories in Stupino to produce Mars and Snickers bars, Uncle Ben's rice and sauces, and Whiskas and Pedigree pet food. As in the past in other European countries, Mars again introduced pet food to a nation that was used to feeding pets its table scraps. In Russia, feeding your dog Pedigree became a high-status concept—like offering your guest a Snickers bar.

Before they sniffed Pedigree and Whiskas, Russian dogs and cats would eat kasha (buckwheat porridge), meat when available, vegetables and bread. When food prices were low, no one minded giving their animals the meal's leftovers. But as prices rose, it started making sense to feed something to pets that cost less than a family's dinner.

Mars used its usual clever advertising to appeal to Russians, who are less sophisticated than their Western counterparts in resisting advertisements' emotional appeals. One Russian woman said, "I started to buy Whiskas [in Russian, pronounced 'Viskas"] because I like this ad. The cat looks so small and unprotected. She can't buy the food herself. I see my cat would buy it if she could, so I buy it for her myself."

However, she mixed Whiskas with kasha.

Mars put $100 million into its plant, one of the most important investments in Russia since the parliamentary elections that pressed for more moderate reform. Russians were pleased with the project: Stupid had been heavily dependent on income derived from producing military components and suffered a high unemployment rate with changes in the country's political and military structure. The country agreed to give Mars a 49-year lease on land south of Moscow.

Not everyone in Russia was pleased to see its "Snickerization." Some resented the way Mars advertised its products before they were available in stores, and disliked the wave of repetitive advertisements that accompanied the candy into the country. People feared that their society was becoming too Western, and was picking up on the ugliest of Western symbols. One cultural critic included Mars candy bars along with handguns on his list deriding trendy Western objects.

As a result, Mars' Masterfoods, once proud to boast of its expansion in Russia, clammed-up and refused to talk about its success in spreading a distribution network across Russia, when so many other Western companies had failed.

Even the *Moskovskaya Pravda* editorialized against Western businesses. "They flooded the country with chocolate bars and now, when you ask schoolchildren to name the planets, they quickly answer, 'Mars, Snickers. . . . '"

## $30 Million or $2.5 Billion

Meanwhile, back in the land of the free and the home of the no-fault divorce. . . .

After Jackie filed for divorce in January 1993, Hank felt she had dumped him like a sack of potatoes. He also felt used: when they first met, Jackie had not only been intrigued by him, she was eager to use him to ease her transition out of marriage to Badger. But Hank realized that now that the bloom was off their relationship, and Jackie was more interested in working for the Mars company, he was thrown aside with no consideration for his feelings nor sensitivity to his recent cancer surgeries.

Hank was also concerned about his future material security. He remembered how, before their marriage, Jackie had promised to take care of him. With that in mind along with a growing awareness of his own health and mortality, he had turned his business, E. Vogel Boots, over to his son and had given his daughter some real estate holdings. By the time Jackie filed for divorce, Hank had retired; his total assets came to perhaps $700,000.

Yet he had signed that prenuptial agreement in 1986 allowing for no support or financial settlement if the couple divorced. Still, in the years following their marriage, Hank had come to realize he had not had a good sense of the extent of Jackie's wealth when he'd signed the agreement. So now he brought the document to an expert, attorney Richard H. Singer Jr. of the New Jersey firm Skoloff & Wolfe, for his opinion.

After studying the agreement, Singer raised serious questions as to its validity. He believed that the agreement and its attached documents had not represented a full and complete disclosure by Jackie of all of her assets, a prerequisite for the legal sustainability of such an agreement. Singer told

Hank that Jackie should have dealt with him in the most forthright and candid manner, since she was asking him to waive all fiduciary rights to her estate. In fact, some experts will advise their clients to disclose more than they are asked to, just to prevent these types of questions from being raised. Yet it seemed to Singer that Jackie had withheld significant information through her financial statement, which said, in part, that she owned shares in Mars, Inc. yet did not disclose what these shares were worth.

Additionally, Singer felt his client had received inadequate counsel from the attorney Hank had hired in 1986 specifically to advise him on the prenuptial agreement. Singer also questioned the discussions that the attorney who drew up Jackie's document had with Hank. "When you're dealing with a premarital agreement," Singer said, "you should avoid having any contact with the person on the other side. Jackie's lawyer had at least three or four conversations with my client during the time the premarital agreement was being negotiated.

"Then Jackie dragged the agreement out and purposely didn't have it produced until shortly before the wedding, quite possibly to put Hank at a significant disadvantage."

Upon close examination, it looked to Singer as if Jackie disguised many, or most, of her assets. Singer thought her financial disclosure would lead one to believe that she might have had a net worth of around $30 million plus interest in some trusts at the time of her marriage. Yet Hank—and Singer—now realized that Jackie owned one-third of Mars, Inc., which puts her assets in the range of several billion dollars.

*Fortune* magazine, for example, had listed the Mars family on its billionaire roster as the fifth wealthiest family in the world. Forbes magazine's annual cover story on the 400 richest Americans—this is the article that had enraged Jackie when she saw her name listed—stated that Jackie, her two brothers and her father together were worth a conservatively estimated $10 billion. It estimated Jackie's personal worth at $2.4 billion. A local business publication, *Business Journal of New Jersey*, cited Jackie as the richest woman in New Jersey, with an individual wealth of at least $1.5 billion—even richer than another well-known New Jersey woman, Doris Duke, had been before her recent death.

How, then, Singer asked, could Jackie's disclosure of perhaps $30 million have been accurate?

Hank and Singer appeared in court in Somerset County, New Jersey, in spring 1992 and alleged that a variety of problems affected the validity of the premarital agreement entered into by Hank and Jackie. To determine Jackie's true wealth, Singer argued before Judge Graham Ross that he must be allowed to review the current financial records and books of Mars, Inc.

Singer said, "My client is alleging that she [Jackie] could have been worth $1 or $2 billion at the time and, if that's true, then this disclosure is fatally flawed and the agreement should be set aside."

Jackie's attorney counter-argued that an accurate value cannot be assigned to Mars, Inc. because it is a private company—although, of course, there are many business experts who would argue to the contrary. In fact, a number of privately held family businesses traditionally are assessed a value, either when there is a death of an owner or when family shareholders want to sell their shares.

Rather than allow Hank and his representatives immediate access to corporate information, Judge Ross decided that the first step to be taken should be to examine the negotiation and execution of the agreement to look for anything which would nullify it.

This means, said Singer, "we are looking at who said what to whom, whether there were any witnesses who were aware of promises made or not made, all the things regarding the negotiation of the agreement and its actual signing. I will then have to make an election as to whether I want to try to convince the judge at this point that I've got enough material to blow out the agreement, or whether I should proceed forward to my request to look at the books and records of Mars, Inc. to see if the disclosure was valid."

As of spring 1995, the case remained at this stage of discovery.

Singer is hopeful that Judge Ross will give him the right to look at the books and records of Mars, Inc. "It seems to me that it would be an integral part of the overall evaluation of the agreement." It is routine in these types of cases, Singer says, "to be allowed to gather all the records together to determine whether the disclosure was full and complete."

## "We Will Just Continue On"— Jackie's lawyer

Jackie is represented by the firm of Courter, Kobert, Laufer, Purcell & Cohen, which has Mars, Inc. as one of its biggest clients, and is located near the large Mars office and plant in Hackettstown, New Jersey. Joel Kobert is not a divorce lawyer—although his partner has done divorce work—but he is leading a team of five other attorneys to represent Jackie. Kobert states categorically that no other member of the Mars family is involved in Jackie's divorce strategizing. In fact, after filing for divorce, Jackie denied in a deposition that she ever told Hank her brothers had been involved in their premarital agreement negotiation.

On the other hand, Hank learned of a comment Jackie's brother Forrest had made regarding the litigation. "Hank is a bad, bad boy," he was to have said.

Hank strongly feels the deck is stacked against him: he has one attorney, whose bills he must pay with his dwindling assets because the court has initially denied him legal fees. Jackie, with no financial concerns, can afford to hire six attorneys, which further lengthens the time the case will take to resolve. Because all the attorneys must be present, scheduling is very difficult.

Hank has said that in late 1991 Jackie's attorneys offered him a settlement of $1 million plus legal fees, which he termed "an insult." Joel Kobert, Jackie's attorney, refused to comment on the alleged offer but in spring of 1995 said that there was going to be no settlement offered to Hank. "We will not, in any way, settle. We think the prenuptial agreement is very clear and there will be no settlement.

"None whatsoever."

Kobert rejected Hank's argument: "What Mr. Vogel is saying is, 'I didn't know she was a wealthy woman.'

"They only dated four or five years and he didn't know? It would be like your telling me that you're going out with someone named Chrysler or Ford and you didn't know they were wealthy," he continued.

"We won't settle because Mr. Vogel is reneging and greedy. What he is saying is, 'I don't care that I was represented by counsel, I don't care that I signed an agreement that was negotiated. I want money.'"

And with this much money at stake, Hank was not surprised to hear from eager reporters covering the divorce. He and Singer, as well as Kobert, gave interviews to *The Washington Post* and *People* magazine, and to a few foreign publications. Additionally, Hank and Singer appeared on *Inside Edition* and *Hard Copy,* and on television shows in Spain and Germany.

Kobert blamed Hank and Singer for the media attention, writing to Judge Ross, "It is no secret that the Defendant and his attorney, Richard Singer, have gone to great efforts to engage the media in this case in an attempt to gain notoriety and perhaps additional business for the firm of Skoloff & Wolfe." He said that Jackie was concerned for her privacy and safety, and for the safety of her adult children, and that there is "no compensation for the agony it has brought upon" Jackie.

Singer responds, "I think this whole thing was raised as a red herring to simply try to stem the flow of any kind of reporting."

He also questions Jackie's real motive in denying Hank a settlement offer that would be taken seriously. "He is not looking to leap into the *Forbes* 400 as a result of this divorce," Singer notes. "What Hank really wants," he says without naming a figure, "would be something that most people would not think twice about in terms of the impact it would have on their net worth."

A friend of Jackie's brothers sympathized not with Jackie, but with Hank. "I hope she doesn't win. She always gets her own way, that Jackie. Her men don't stand a chance, do they?"

The case drags on, reminding Hank of way Jackie threatened to destroy him, he says, by spinning the litigation out as long as possible. The balance of power and wealth is on her side.

Jackie's attorney feels it will take perhaps until 1997 to be over, at least five years from the time she filed for divorce. Kobert says, "It will continue because we are not going to settle. We will just continue on."

## "The Company . . . Must be a Good Citizen"— Hershey

Despite their tremendous wealth, none of the Marses —neither Forrest Sr. nor any of his three children—have been lauded for their philanthropy. The Mars Foundation, with Jackie as president and Forrest Jr. and John as vice presidents, uses the corporation's Elm Street address as its headquarters. In 1993, the foundation, which is funded by Mars, Inc., had total assets of close to $5 million. That year, the company had estimated sales of $8.5 billion but gave only $600,000 to its foundation, a paltry gift considering the wealth of the company and of its owners.

Mars family members are noticeably absent from any roster of major philanthropic donors. *Town and Country* magazine periodically publishes a list of "Super Santas," the nation's most generous citizens. The write-up includes such families as the Annenbergs, the Rockefellers, the Mellons, the Nielsens, the Albrittons and the Haases. Nowhere to be found are any members of the Mars family, who are actually wealthier than nearly all the people who have given so generously.

Compare, for example, the $70.5 million gift that Harvard University is to receive in 1995 from John L. and Frances Lehman Loeb to the $15,000 gift that the Mars Foundation made to Yale University in 1993.

Look too at other gifts to universities in the 90s: $64 million given to Florida State University by the Appleton family; $15 million donated to the University of California at Berkeley (where Forrest Sr. spent several of his undergraduate years) by Ann and Gordon Getty; $21 million gifted to Princeton University by Laurance S. Rockefeller; and $13.5 million given to the College of Idaho from the Albertsons. Then look at the largest gift of the Mars Foundation in 1993 to an institution of higher learning: $105,500 to Wheaton College.

To contrast further the Mars gift-giving record to the good works of others, look at the efforts the company that revolutionized the world's rice-eating habits using the image of a fictional African-American man made toward helping with the education of African-American students. In the same period that the Mars foundation gave $5,000 to the Black Student Fund, Walter Annenberg gave $50 million to the United Negro College Fund.

The largest donation the foundation made in 1992, for example, was $100,000; the smallest was $1,000. Its typical gifts that year ranged from $2,000 to $15,000. Many of its donations benefit the schools that Jackie, Forrest or John attended. To the elementary and secondary independent schools that the Marses and their children have attended go the types of checks that are written out by many professional couples who have enrolled their children in private school: not the sizable donations that one expects from billionaires. Chatham Hall, Madeira School and Holton Arms School each received $1,000, for example, while Foxcroft School got $4,000.

Organizations that battle cancer, the cause Audrey Mars held so dear, glean more from the Mars foundation than any other medical societies. Even there, the foundation contributes comparatively little: only $31,000, total, was donated to such groups as the American Cancer Society and the Cancer Research Institute.

Wildlife and environmental groups benefit from the Mars foundation, but not by any great sums. The Chesapeake Bay Foundation received $10,000 and the Ruffled Grouse Society, of which Hank Vogel is a board member, received $5,000.

Philanthropic boards whose members have appointed the Mars siblings as directors in the hope of receiving a major contribution have been disappointed. Forrest Jr. was named to the board of American University in Washington, D.C. No major contribution was made; the gift that university received from the Mars Foundation in 1993 was a scant $5,000. Nor was Forrest at the forefront of any university fundraising effort that would have brought in contributions from others.

"The brothers are simply not eleemosynary inclined," notes one Washington civic leader, in reference to their stinginess. "They have focused their attention on their business and that seems to be the be-all and the end-all of their lives."

Several of the Mars wives have done what they could to compensate for their husbands' lack of benevolence. Audrey, who had a fortune bestowed on her from her husband, had her own charities and gave enormous amounts to international efforts and cancer research. When Virginia was married to Forrest Jr., fellow board members felt she was disappointed by her husband's penurious ways and perhaps even embarrassed that she and Forrest were not contributing more to the organizations to which she gave her time. Still, "She could never bring Forrest along with her," says one fellow board member. "She ran up against a brick wall."

Following Virginia's divorce, she remained a leader in the National Symphony Orchestra. As a board member, she personally would be expected to give a minimum of $25,000 and to help raise more. At least, now, with her $50 million divorce settlement, she is free to contribute as she desires.

Mars, Inc. is not the only business headquartered in metropolitan Washington that is myopic when it comes to local philanthropy. Austin Kiplinger, chairman of The Kiplinger

Washington Editors, Inc. and one of Washington's most active philanthropists and civic leaders, points out that many national organizations "don't particularly want to be conspicuously identified with Washington."

He explains, "Washington is not popular and it never has been. The chronic attitude of Americans toward Washington is that it is evil. Many corporations are here to be influential and get in on the lobbying but don't want anybody to know they're here."

Nevertheless, several regional families—most notably the Cafritz family of the real estate and development firm, the Meyer family of *The Washington Post* and the Kiplinger publishing family—have established foundations that have positively affected the daily lives of their fellow Washingtonians. These families have values that resemble those of Milton Hershey.

On the other hand, the Marriott family of the hotel company contributes relatively little to the area. Neither Mobil Corporation, which is in Fairfax County, Virginia, near the Mars company, and which is the fourth largest petroleum business in the world, nor Martin Marietta Corporation, the aerospace and chemical business that is located in Bethesda, Maryland, are known as major donors. But even in this chilly atmosphere, Mars, Inc. is an extreme example of tightfistedness.

Other well-known candy families, such as the Gordons of Tootsie Roll Industries, reflect strong philanthropic traditions. The Gordons, for example, are heavy contributors to health care and medical research. So, if the Mars company and its owners are set side by side to either competing candy businesses or to area Washington firms, they compare unfavorably.

Nor do the Marses compensate for local stinginess by generosity farther afield. At various times, company representatives have claimed that Mars, Inc. has given millions of dollars to charities worldwide. These gifts are anonymous so the company won't be besieged by requests, the company says. Yet one area philanthropist—who was reluctant to be named—commented, "I would question that. If they've given anything substantial, it would be known. So I think that's a bit of a dodge."

Even assuming that there are in fact large gifts made—and research turns up none—it is important for an individual or a company to take a public position so that others are aware that philanthropy is seen by community and business leaders as an essential role. Richard Berezden—the former president of American University, who structured tremendous growth at that school during his tenure—talked Forrest Mars Jr. into serving on the American University board in the 80s. But in the event, Forrest disappointed the board. Berezden says, "Ideally, you would like to have a person who is prominent, who is known for philanthropy, who gives money and who publicly says so. That's a dream combination.

"Having someone visibly listed, either on the board or as a part of the fund-raising effort, who is known in the community as a person of substantial means, sends a message to others that this is important, big-league work. When someone doesn't want to have his name listed, it's not as helpful."

Another Washingtonian who has known all of the Mars men, described Forrest Jr. and John as "almost recluses in this town," who would shy away from civic work.

Although it is not uncommon for an individual to give an anonymous gift, why would a corporation give a gift anonymously? Hershey's chairman, Ken Wolfe, seemed perplexed when asked about any anonymous contributions that Hershey had made, since there is no reason for a corporation to disguise its name when making a donation. He said, on the contrary, "We don't do anything anonymously. The company has always felt that we must be a good citizen. We have plants scattered all around the United States and we try to be a contributor to all the communities in which we have plants."

Additionally, Hershey encourages its employees to be active in philanthropies and non-profit organizations. As a company, it sponsors the National Track & Field Youth Program and supports the Children's Miracle Network, which benefits hundreds of children's hospitals throughout the country. In addition, Wolfe says, "As a general company policy, we do encourage people to get involved and so we always have someone from our company serving on the school board or involved with the local township committee or something like that. We obviously try to accommodate them so that they can do these things."

Tootsie Roll, also, likes to see its employees become involved in their community. "We encourage it, obviously," says Ellen Gordon. "Many of our people are interested in philanthropic work. We have one manager who is very involved with the Spina Bifida Association."

In contrast, Mars prohibits its associates from having their photographs taken for publication and stresses that they must keep a low profile, even outside the company. These policies would not lend themselves to encouraging a staff member to serve on a school board, for example. The Mars rules severely inhibit the opportunity for employees to make major contributions to their community. And the Mars philosophy that winning in business is paramount over all other concerns certainly does little to encourage employees to take time to volunteer for charitable organizations.

Even when the Mars family members do use their names, the gifts are often small. Washington's National Symphony

Orchestra was let down by board member Virginia Mars, Forrest Jr.'s first wife, because she initially had to be pressured into contributing money to the symphony drive—though her more generous impulses may have been being squeezed by Forrest.

Nor will the company join the civic groups that do so much to improve communities and encourage economic growth. Mars, even though it is metropolitan Washington's largest private business, has refused to join the Greater Washington Board of Trade, unlike other area companies.

And both Forrest Jr. and John are not involved in working for the good of the confectionery business as a whole. Ellen Gordon has a high profile among candy leaders, having been active in their organizations and in organizations that promote women managers. "I think it's important to support the confectionery industry and to give people a chance to network and talk about areas of mutual interest."

But just like their father, neither Forrest Jr. or John share this point of view. Both are distant to others in the industry. "They are more involved in their own business and they don't participate so much in the outside industry," Gordon notes.

The differences between Mars founder Frank and his son Forrest Sr., and Hershey Foods founder Milton Hershey, are especially telling. The establishment of Milton Hershey School has meant that literally tens of thousands of children have been housed and educated since the first four boys were enrolled in 1910. Before his death, Milton Hershey also founded Hershey Junior College, which has since merged with Harrisburg Area Community College.

In addition, to commemorate Milton Hershey's belief in the value of education, the Hershey Trustees funded The Milton S. Hershey Medical Center. Trust board directors asked the president of Penn State to attend a meeting with them, at which they asked him if that Penn State needed a medical school. The president agreed but said that the state could not afford to fund one. The Hershey people asked, "How much would it take?" The president answered, "$50 million." The Hershey response was, "We think we can get it."

Milton Hershey believed in giving back to the community where he lived. Forrest Mars Sr.'s main residence for more than 40 years was Marland, in The Plains area. This Virginia region has benefited greatly from having been the choice of the wealthy for country homes. But Forrest's estate has never even been open for the Hunt Country Stable Tour, as have been the Randolph farms, Jack Kent Cooke's Fallingbrook estate, the Woffords' Fox Covert Farm or Paul Mellon's Rokeby stables.

The Mellon family probably has been the most generous benefactors of the area. Paul contributed hundreds of millions of dollars to the Old Dominion Foundation, which assists communities and organizations throughout the state. In Upperville, close to Forrest's Marland, the Mellons also constructed the Trinity Episcopal Church, and did not stint on quality. Trinity has been called the most beautiful rural church in America, as it was built in the style of medieval cathedrals by world-famous artists and artisans. Bunny Mellon spends a considerable amount of time helping Trinity Church—where, by the way, Forrest Sr. was a member but never an important donor.

The Harper family, of Harper & Row publishing, have always been noted for their gifts to the area, as have the Fleischmann margarine family and the Howell Jackson family, who built the area's community center. But neither Forrest nor his daughter Jackie, who now has her own nearby estate Stonehall Farm, have been known to give anything worth noting to the community.

With one exception: Hunt country residents do remember that when they were children attending Trinity Church Christmas parties in the 50s, they received M&M's donated by Forrest Sr.

Mars gifts melt in the mouth . . . and in the pocket.

# Eight

# The Future of Mars

Just as Jackie and her retinue of attorneys will continue on, so will Mars, Inc. While the fifth largest private company in the United States is hardly about to crash out of orbit, its future remains cloudy. By the mid-90s, Mars had fallen even further behind Hershey Foods, its strongest competitor in the North American confectionery field. Hershey wisely planned such acquisitions as the purchase of Peter Paul Cadbury, and they have paid off handsomely for the company, while Forrest Jr. and John Mars bite their nails at the thought of incurring any significant debt, whatever the prospects for profit down the road. Mars has not bought another company since the mid-80s addition of Forrest Sr.'s tiny Ethel M and the then-profitable Dove International—which it quickly turned to a loss.

Hershey is targeting its new products—both line extensions and innovations—so that these introductions do not cannibalize its core brands. By comparison, Mars has been only partly successful with its new me-too imitation products. Those candy bars that were popular ate into sales of the core Mars lines. Sales of line extensions of well-known brands do well initially, but then fall off in sales. The gap between Hershey and Mars has been widening since the early 90s, to Hershey's benefit.

This is why Hershey's 1994 United States market share was 26.6 percent, according to Food Data Base. Mars was holding at 23.2 percent, with Nestlé a distant third in the United States at ten percent. Although Mars' Snickers bar and Hershey's Reese's Peanut Butter Cup continued to vie for the number one spot, the most popular branded chocolate candy bar of 1994's top ten was Snickers, according to a spokesperson for *Confectionery Magazine.* Second was Reese's Peanut Butter Cups and third and fourth were M&M's Plain and M&M's Peanut Chocolate Candies. In fifth place was Hershey's Kisses, sixth was Hershey's Kit Kat bar, seventh was Mars' Milky Way, and in the next two spots were Hershey's Milk Chocolate Bar With Almonds and Hershey's Nuggets With Almonds. Tying for tenth place were Hershey's Milk Chocolate bar and Hershey's Nuggets. Hershey had six of the top ten bars, of which three were relatively recent (Kit Kat and the two varieties of Nuggets). Mars had four of the top ten bars, all of them mature brands.

In Europe, where Hershey barely has a presence, such enormous global companies as Nestlé, Cadbury Schweppes and Philip Morris are gobbling up smaller companies and growing stronger every day. Meanwhile, Mars is losing significant market share in countries where it had been the center of the candy universe. True, it has swallowed a great part of the Russian candy market. But its financial losses in the United Kingdom are shocking.

Because the company is private, it is able to keep its losses closer to the vest than a public company could. There are other benefits to being privately held, mostly the ability to concentrate on the long-term and not have to sweat quarterly results. Of course, to the secretive Mars family, being able to withhold financial information is a joy of its own.

One of the most striking characteristics of Mars, Inc. is that it is such a large company for one so closely held. When a company is as tightly held as Mars, managed by its owners, there are virtually no outside stockholders to whom the managers must be accountable. One can only surmise that if Forrest Jr. and John had been held responsible for their decisions of the past decade, they would not have been able to persist in operating as they have, and would have received a wake-up call from shareholders before they continued to slide down the slope of market share attrition.

Whenever the company's orbit wobbles, and a public comment must be made, the Mars spin is that the blip does not matter: the concern is in business for the long haul. That cloud cover is wearing thin. In fact, Mars has been making some awfully big mistakes and, eventually, its erratic course will send it crashing. What smokescreen will its spokesperson send up then?

The brothers also need to learn how to turn an operation around and make it profitable as soon as it starts to falter. As one associate said, "You are taught nothing about failure at Mars. It is win, win, win all the time." The company must become more flexible and figure out how to turn defeat around on those occasions when it cannot "win."

Each year for the past decade, it has experienced serious losses. Its senior managers are leaving in droves and there is a paucity of new ideas coming from those who are left behind, partly because staff are too fearful of Forrest and John to venture innovative opinions.

Additionally, the company's execution of new product introductions has been mangled. Although the brothers have recognized this and have tried to deal with these issues by forming endless task forces, the company's problems with supply and distribution led the *Times* of London in 1994 to describe Mars as in "terminal decline." No one is confident that Forrest or John can regain the supremacy in candy or pet food that Mars once enjoyed. Also in 1994, the weekly marketing newsletter *The Delaney Report* highlighted the company's problems and gave its Quarterly Award for Worst Marketer to Forrest Jr.:

> For allowing the company to continue to lose ground to competitor Hershey Foods in the candy marketplace. For not being aggressive enough in developing new brands with long-lasting impact. For a series of management turnovers in the important M&M/Mars candy unit that has led to a lingering morale problem.

Again, unlike in a public company, executives in private family-owned businesses must adapt to the dynamics of that family. For the Mars managers, that means they must deal with brothers who are autocratic, controlling, cold rivals, and who have delegated their younger sister to run around the world making amends for their shortcomings in interpersonal skills.

There's also the considerable history to this clan, that Mars associates quickly pick up on. In the previous generation, Forrest Sr., fought over the company with his own father Frank and with his step-mother. The founding generation's legacy of emotional distance and control was inherited by Forrest Sr. He displayed these characteristics through surprise attacks on his adult sons, who never knew why or when their father was going to blow up. That's why Mars associates have learned never to mention Forrest Sr.'s name to the brothers.

Forrest Jr. and John, too, behave as autocratically and dictatorially toward others as their own father did toward them. Although they can be fiery with rage, underneath that hot surface their cores are frozen.

They must know that they are disliked by many managers when they see Mars associates anonymously quoted, for example, in Bill Saporito's 1994 *Fortune* magazine article, saying, "The Mars brothers are shits."

Since they trust no one, they have come to rely on sycophants within the organization who tell them what they want to hear. The advice the brothers subsequently hear has often proven unwise.

The brothers try to appear less concerned than they apparently are about the company's downward trend. They will point to the new, potentially huge, markets being carved out for Mars in such places as China and Russia. Yet, very soon, even this growth will end as they run out of new countries to introduce their mature brands to. What then? Perhaps an interplanetary market will open up.

But it had better do so soon. Forrest Jr. is now 64 years old and John is approaching 60. Both men are as old as Forrest Sr. was when he finally wrested control of Frank's Mars candy company from his stepmother and her half brother in 1964 and merged it with M&M's and his other firms. Over the years, Forrest Sr. has frequently reminded his sons how much he had accomplished by the time he was their ages—and taunted them that they have done less, with more, than he.

Recently, he remarked bitterly to a man about his sons' management of the company he gave them. "They think they can't run it into the ground—but they can," said Forrest Sr.

His derision has had its effect on his sons. John lost his temper recently when the siblings and their spouses had gathered and were talking about the father. John was furious to realize that he was nearly 60 and still worrying about his father's reaction. "That crazy old man," he screamed at the astonished group.

The brothers also clashed with their father during a crucial discussion with Nestlé in the early 90s. The hungry global giant was in distant third place in the United States confectionery market, behind Hershey and Mars. Although it could hope to advance gradually by gobbling up little candy companies, it could vault itself into first place in market share by simply buying a company that already had a larger one: Mars, Inc. By combining its approximately 10 percent market share with Mars' huge domestic percentage, Nestlé would in one move rid itself of competition with Mars and hop over Hershey to take the confectionery lead. The merger would also add to Nestlé's ice cream strength in the United States, which the company had been fueling through such 90s acquisitions as the Drumstick Company and Eskimo Pie Corp., and through manufacturing and marketing of Dole brand Fruit 'n' Juice bars and other frozen snacks. Additionally, the Mars buy would move Nestlé closer to the European front rank in both candy and ice cream.

The talks between Mars and Nestlé began in the fall of 1991 and continued into early 1992. Mars originally refused to respond to press queries about the proposed merger, while Nestlé flat out denied it was in merger talks at all. "There are no negotiations going on with Mars," a Nestlé spokesperson said from the home office in Switzerland. But when asked if "discussions," rather than "negotiations," were taking place between the Mars family and Nestlé, the spokesperson confirmed the talks. Then he demurred, "That is as far as I'm prepared to go."

Under persistent press probing, Mars was finally forced to comment. An associate said, in typically terse Mars style, "There is absolutely no truth in that."

According to the Swiss business weekly *Schweizerische Handeleszeitung*, the Mars family initiated a visit with Helmut Maucher, Nestlé's chief executive, because they were worried about succession at the company. This story is confirmed by an attendee at the gathering where the buy-out was discussed at length by Forrest Sr., his sons and his daughter.

Forrest Sr. seriously wanted to consider selling. After all, in his long life, Forrest had never explicitly ruled out the possibility of selling Mars or turning it public. In fact, as he aged, he increasingly expressed regret that he had given his children a business with $500 million in revenue that had no significant debt. He would "never do it again. Not turn it over to his kids, anyway," reported a man who had heard this discussion.

This type of talk, of course, is not what his children wanted to hear, having spent their lifetimes at the company. As they contemplated the prospect of selling the business, they focused on concern about their posterity. Should Mars, Inc. be handed to the fourth generation, lock, stock and barrel, as it had been given to Forrie, John and Jackie by their father?

Of the ten young adults in the new generation, seven have worked for the company. All four of Forrest's daughters—Victoria, Pamela, Valeria and Marijke—have worked there, as have John's children—Linda, Mike and Frank. (Although John named his last child after his grandfather, founder of the Mars empire, none of Forrest Sr.'s children named any of their offspring after him.)

The only cousins who have openly declared that they wanted no part of careers at Mars are Jackie's older children, Alexandra and Steve. And though Jackie's youngest, Christa, is only 20 years old and still in school, it does not appear that she will break ranks with her siblings. After all, these three young people have had both parents—Jackie, and their father David Badger—entangled in Mars, Inc., and they have seen what the company has done to them.

Among the remaining Mars cousins, no one in the family has identified a successor strong enough to pull this company back up to where it once was. "None of them are capable of it," says someone who knows the cousins. Apparently, even Forrest Jr. and John recognize that none of their children has shown, as yet, the special talents and instincts needed by the head of a global business. They also may lack the ambition needed to head a multinational corporation; after all, they are trust fund kids.

Nor has anyone within the company identified a future leader. Quite the opposite: one associate at Ethel M remarked on John's son Frank to a reporter with *Las Vegas Business Press.* When the reporter asked about Frank's job duties, the associate, pinned to the wall, stuttered, "Technically, he's in charge of . . . he's part of the family."

In any case, the proposed merger was blocked: although Jackie appeared willing to sell, neither Forrest Jr. nor John wanted to sell Mars, Inc. to Nestlé. What would they do with the rest of their lives, if they did sell? At their ages, they had no desire to work for other people within a giant corporation. Nor did they have any entrepreneurial spark that might interest them in taking the money and starting a new company, as did Craig McCaw after the McCaw Cellular Communications buyout by AT&T. The Mars company had been their lives, especially to workaholic John.

He particularly resisted selling the company because he was looking forward to his older brother's retirement. The plan was for Forrest Jr. to leave John at the helm of the company. After all, although the men were co-presidents of the company, Forrest alone had been chairman and chief executive officer. John wanted to try those titles on for size, without his tall brother around.

And the specter of being swallowed by a giant rival still stalks the Mars halls. Franois Perroud, vice president of Nestlé, spoke from Switzerland to refute the notion of a merger. "There's no way in the world where, in any large market, you could conceive of a combination of both Nestlé and Mars. It's not going to be accepted. Here, clearly, not in one single instance could such a thing be tolerated. Not in any large market. Perhaps in a small one, but who cares if you have 100 percent of the Andoran chocolate market?"

Perroud says he has been fighting off the Mars-Nestlé merger stories since the initial article appeared in Switzerland in late 1991. "I know the person wrote the story simply because he saw Mr. Forrest Mars Jr. and my boss [Helmut Maucher, Nestlé's chief executive] at a lunch table and he came up with this totally groundless speculation."

Perroud at first denied that the two men had talked about a possible merger at all. Then, when told that there was a witness to the family discussions, he quickly backed down and did not deny that the topic could have been raised at the luncheon table and that there could have been follow-up talks within the Mars family about a buyout. He still maintained, "Even if it were a serious discussion, it still does not alter the facts. It does not depend solely on the will of either party to be a purchaser or to be a buyer. It simply depends on the given fact that anti-competitive legislation today would not allow us to make the merger.

"And I am convinced that both Mr. Mars and, certainly, my boss are realists enough to realize it can't be done."

For whatever reason, within the Mars family, talks about Nestlé petered out. And since then, Mars Inc. has been moving in the wrong direction.

Forrest Sr., titan of business, through age and poor health, has been relegated to the role of docile old man. On March 21, 1995, for Forrest's ninety-first birthday, Jackie flew down to Florida to celebrate with him. She took the old man to Sea World, walking by the side of his wheelchair as the attendant pushed it, pointing out the dolphins and the whales.

# Epilogue

# The Farewell

By 1994, Forrest Sr. was starting to fail. He had suffered several strokes and had difficulty supporting himself when he stood; he could no longer walk more than a few feet. A physical therapist was working with him every day. His hearing was poor, cutting him off further from communication with his children, since he had such a hard time hearing them on the telephone.

But there was one thing he wanted to do. He wanted to go back to The Plains one last time. When he had moved from the flat above the Ethel M plant in Henderson, Nevada to north Miami, he had also sold Marland, although he retained Audrey's old Watergate apartment. So when he returned to the area that meant so much to him, he stayed in Jackie's new Stonehall Farm—only a few miles from the old Zulla intersection fronting Marland where, decades earlier, he had built concrete-block houses for his farm workers.

Stonehall Farm was comfortable, and he surely enjoyed visiting with Jackie. But that, evidently, was not why he had made the long trip.

At his request, Jackie called for the car. Its driver assisted the doddering patriarch out of the wheelchair and into the back seat. The driver got behind the wheel, and, following Forrest's instructions, drove the old man through The Plains, then through Upperville and on through Middleburg.

Forrest sat, gazing out the window, remembering.

# Index